Mandalas Sketchbook
Free coloring pages

Nina Packer

Mandalas Sketchbook

Polar graph
Free coloring pages

ISBN-13: 978-1718932166

ISBN-10: 1718932162

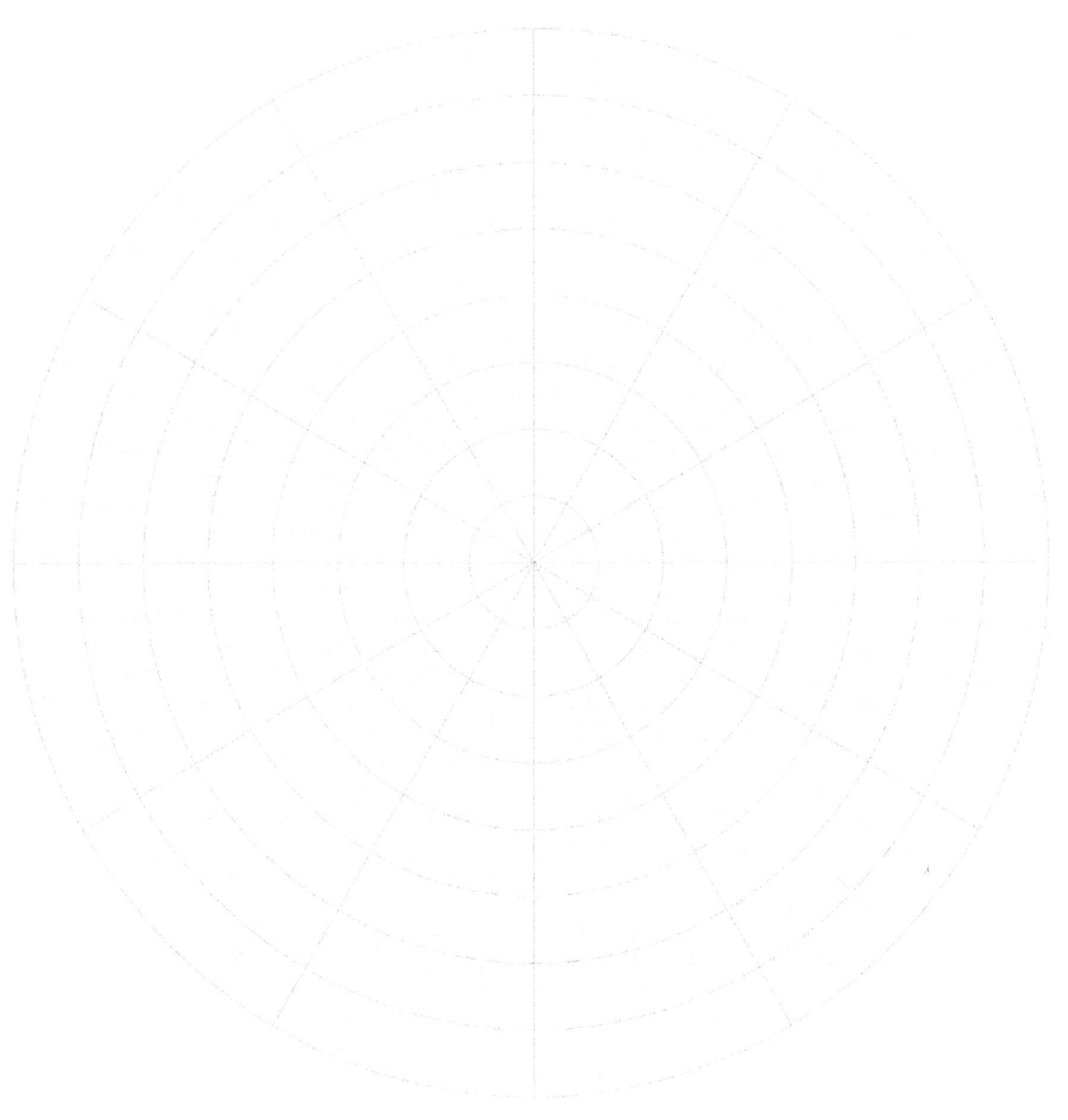

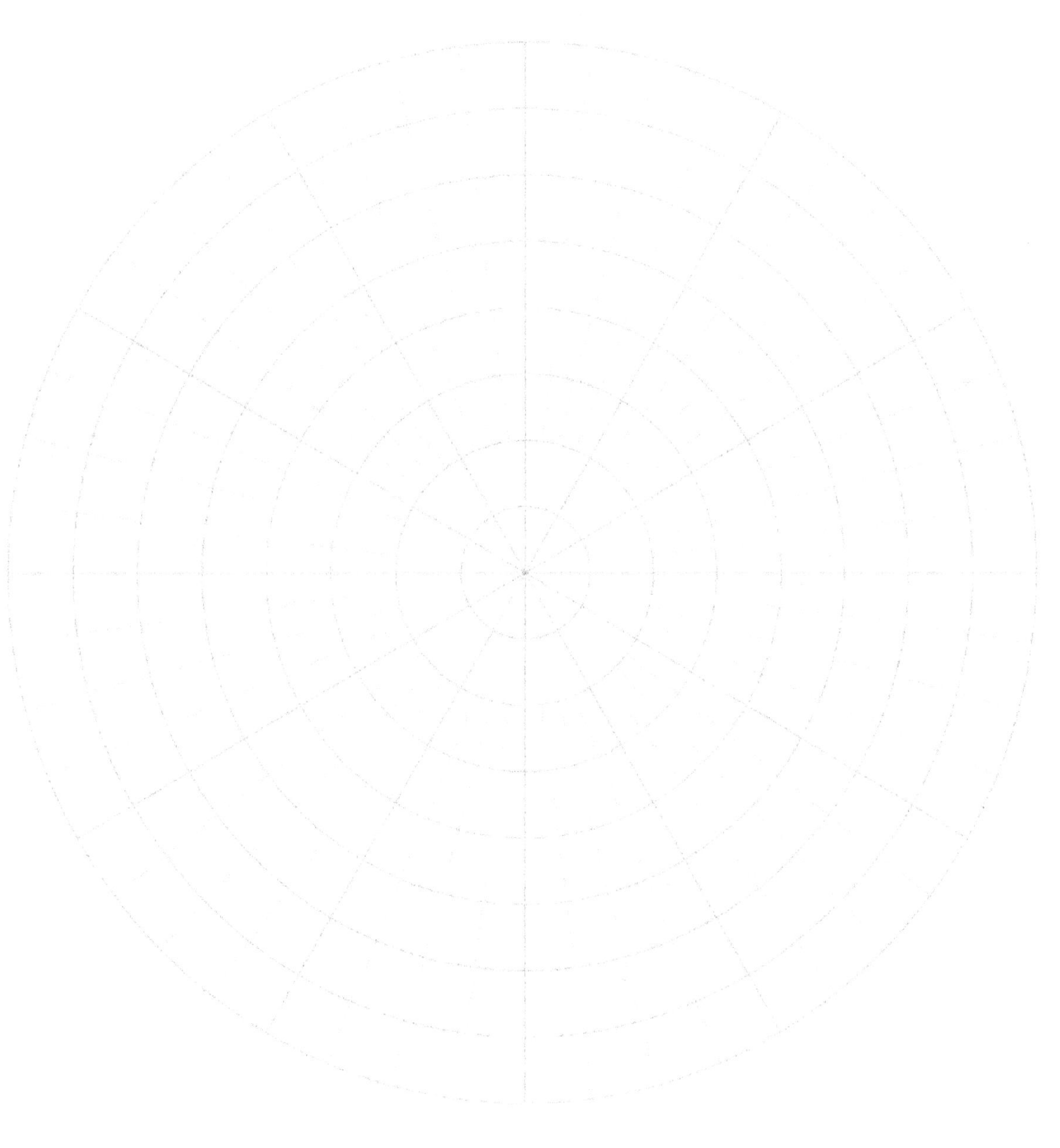

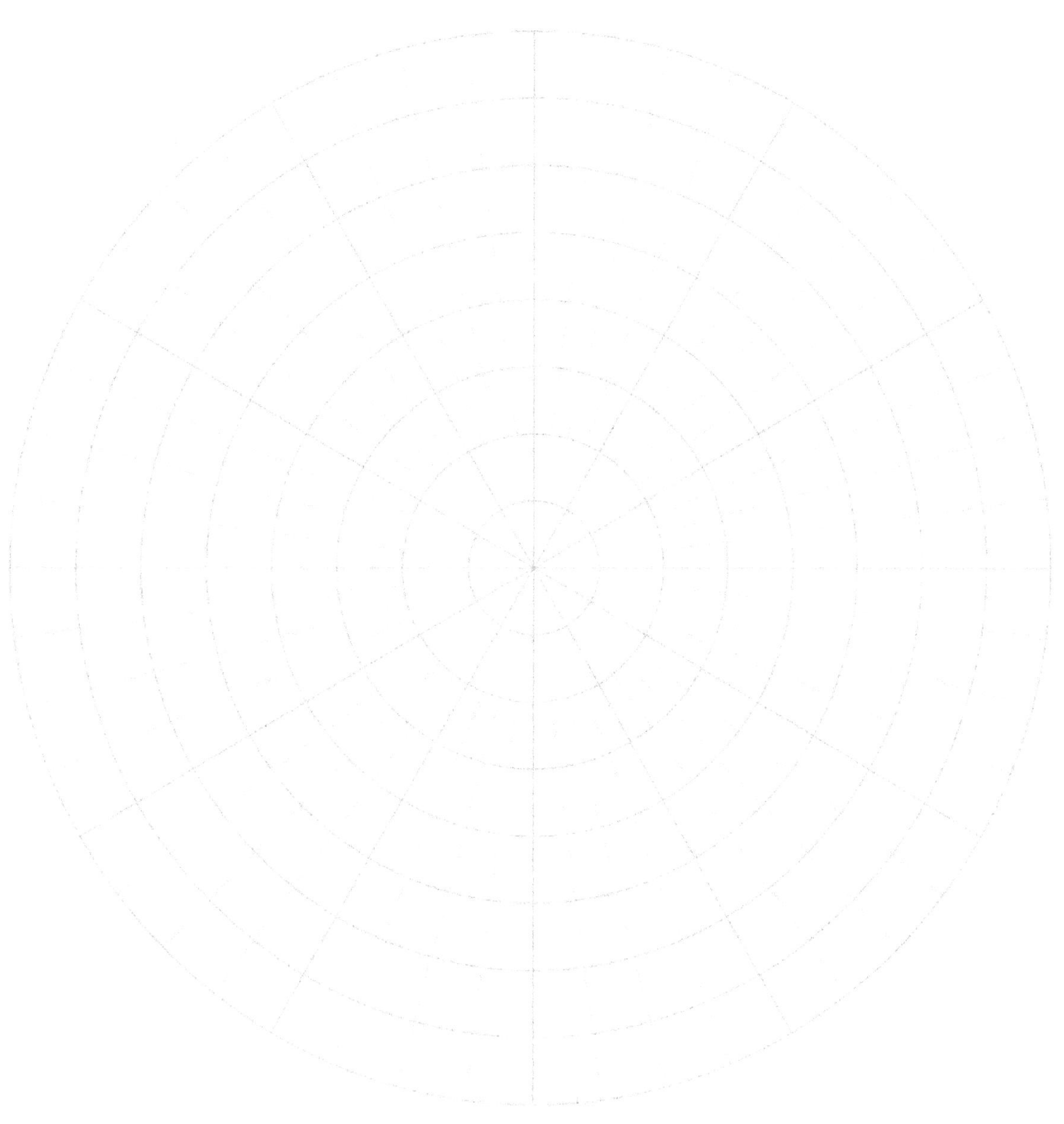

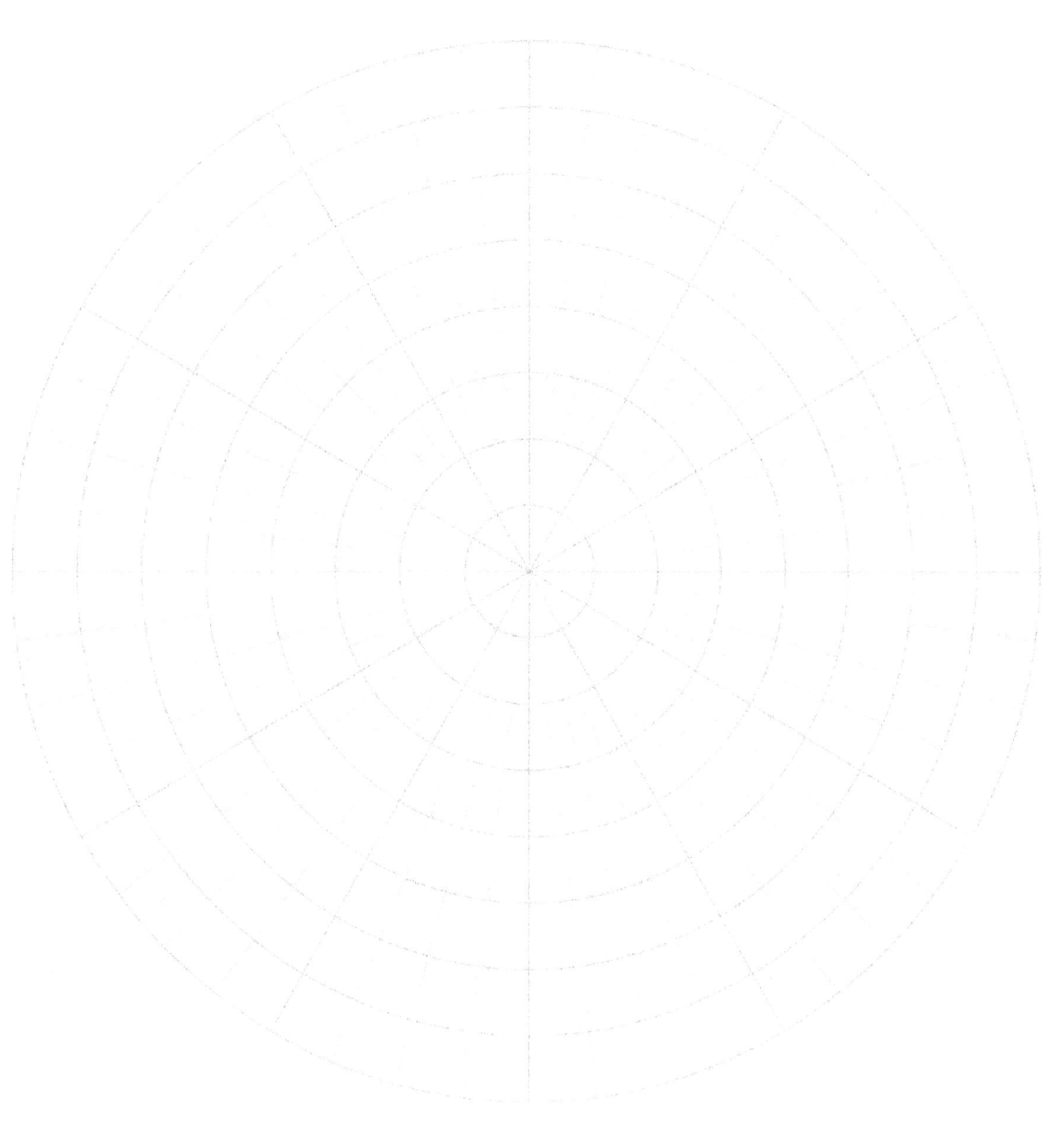

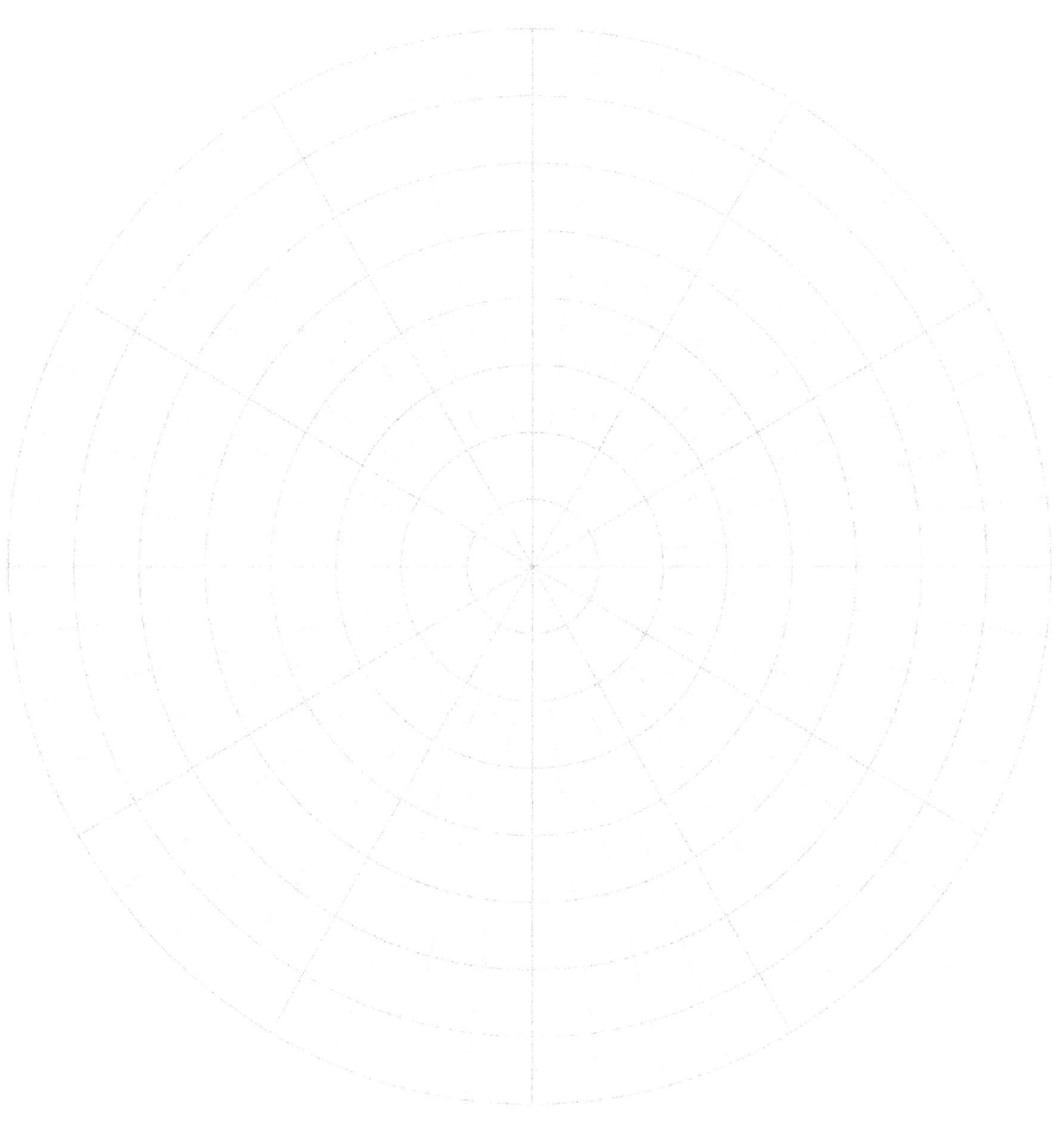

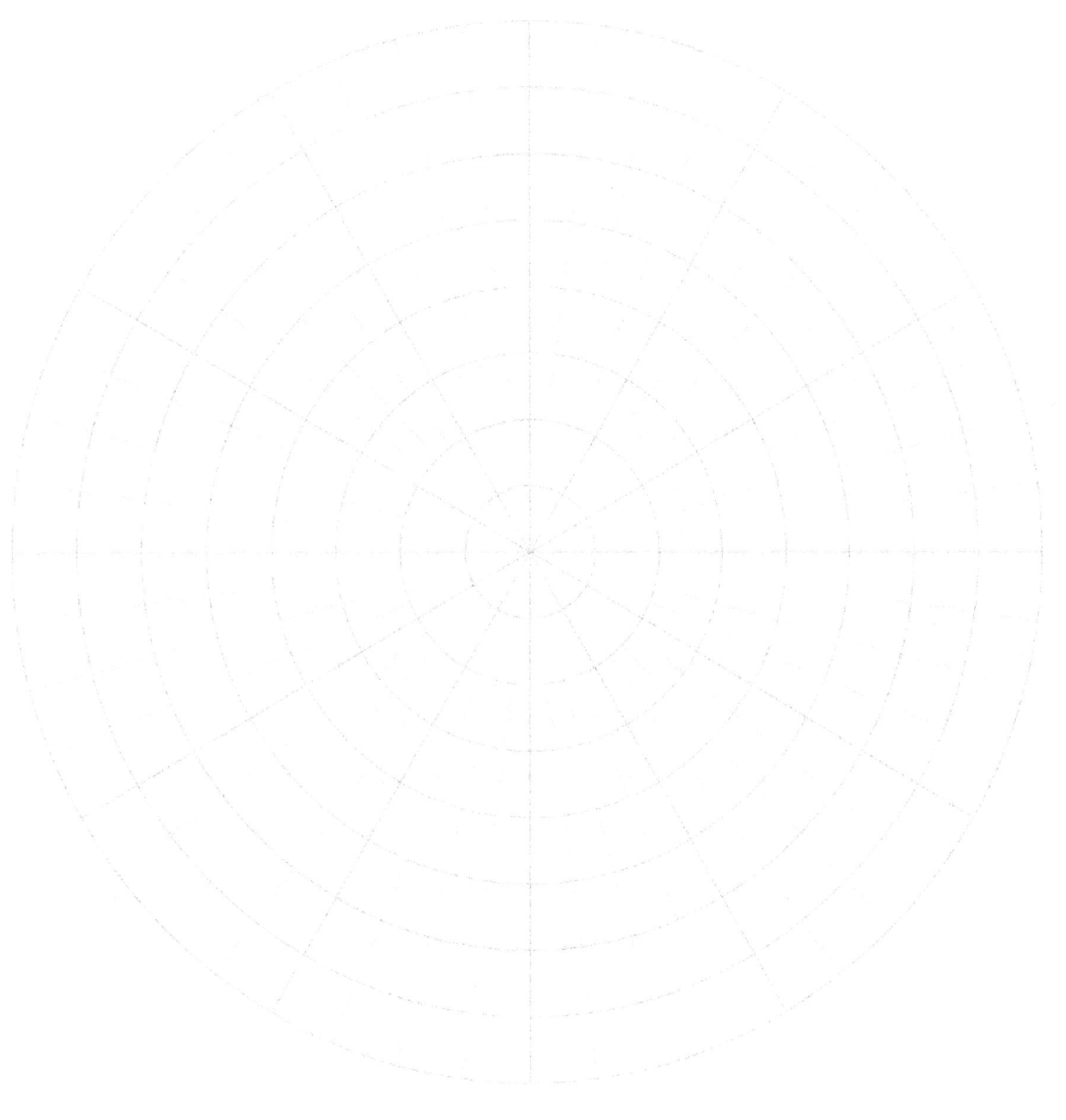

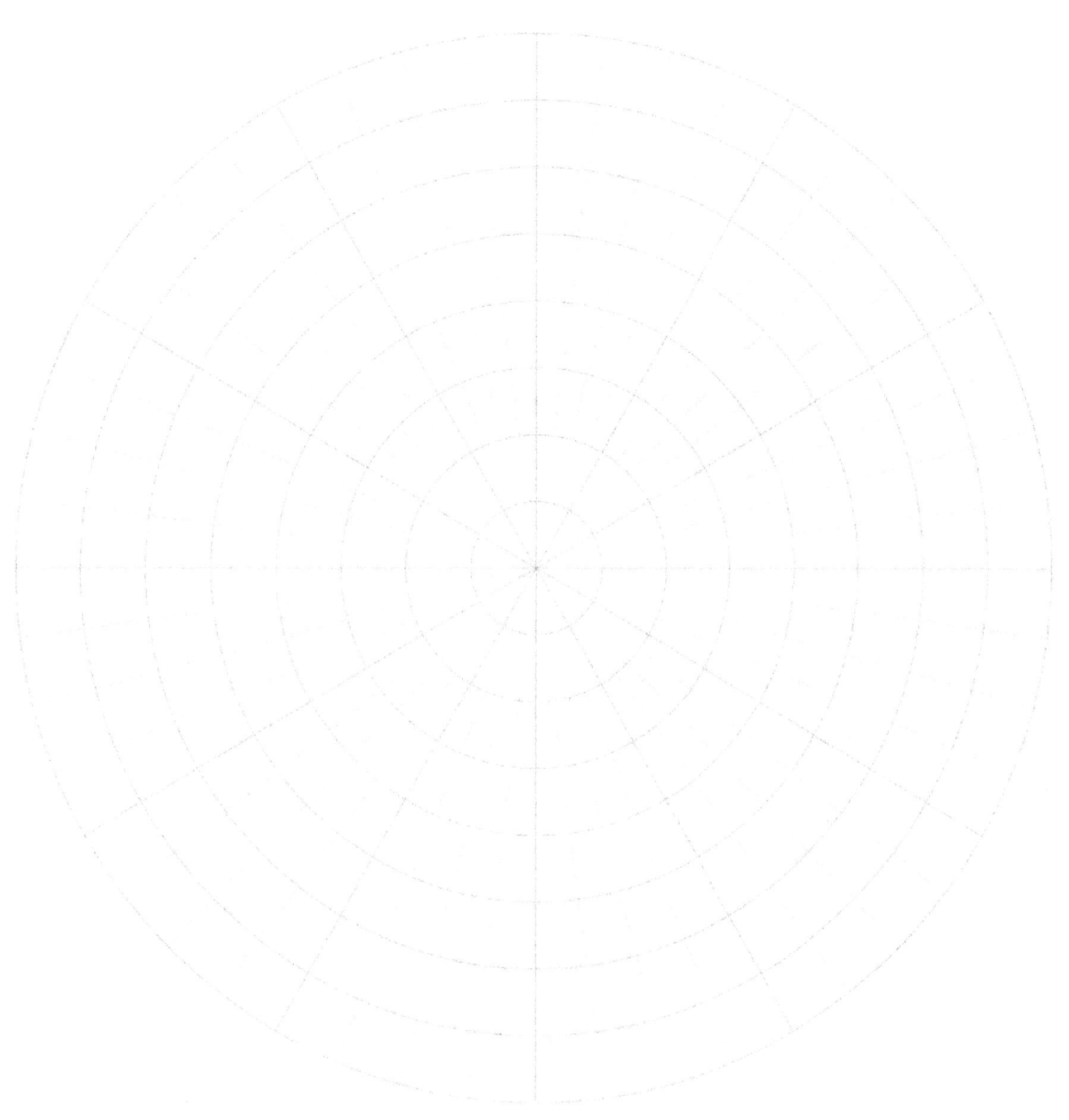

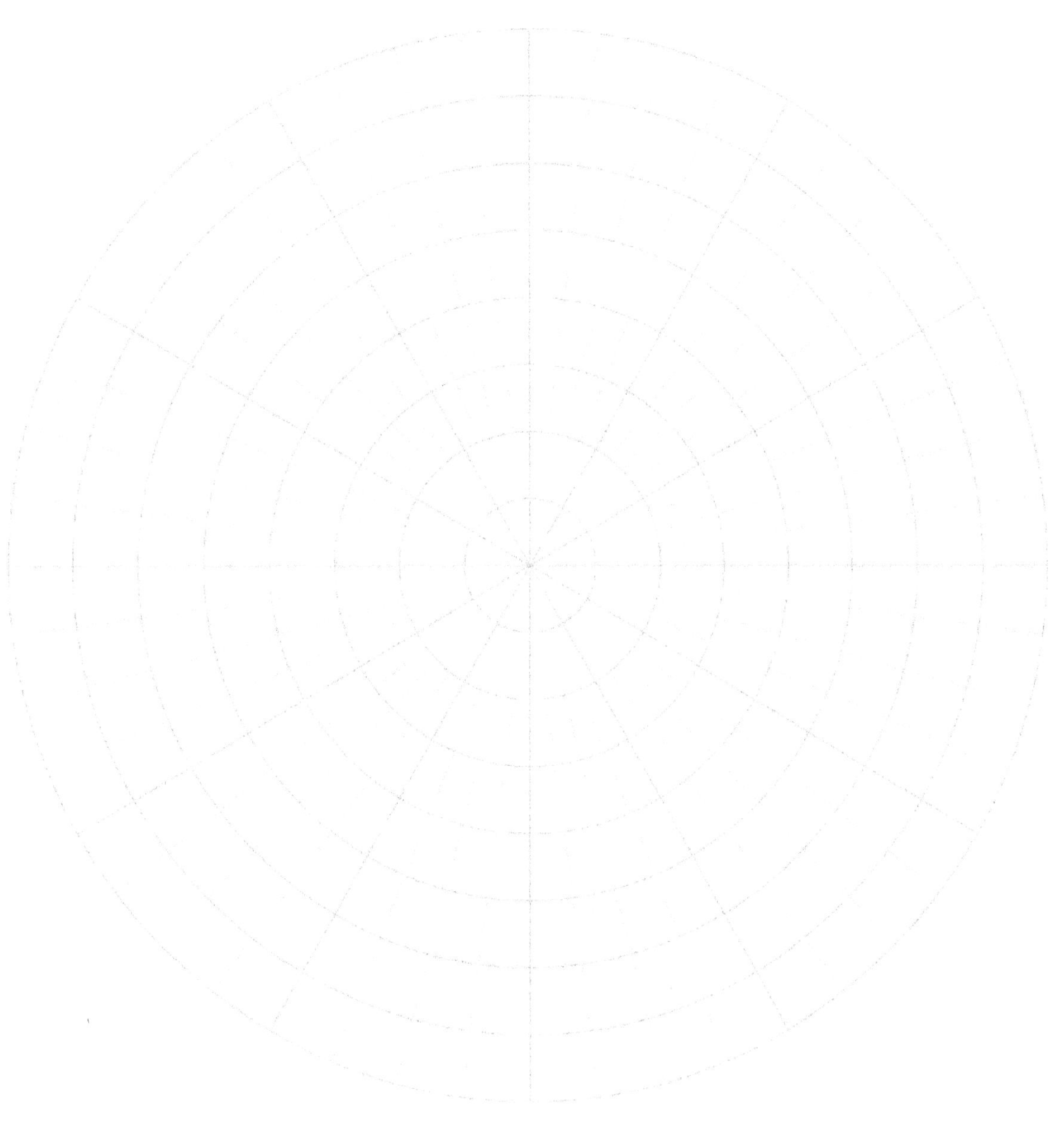

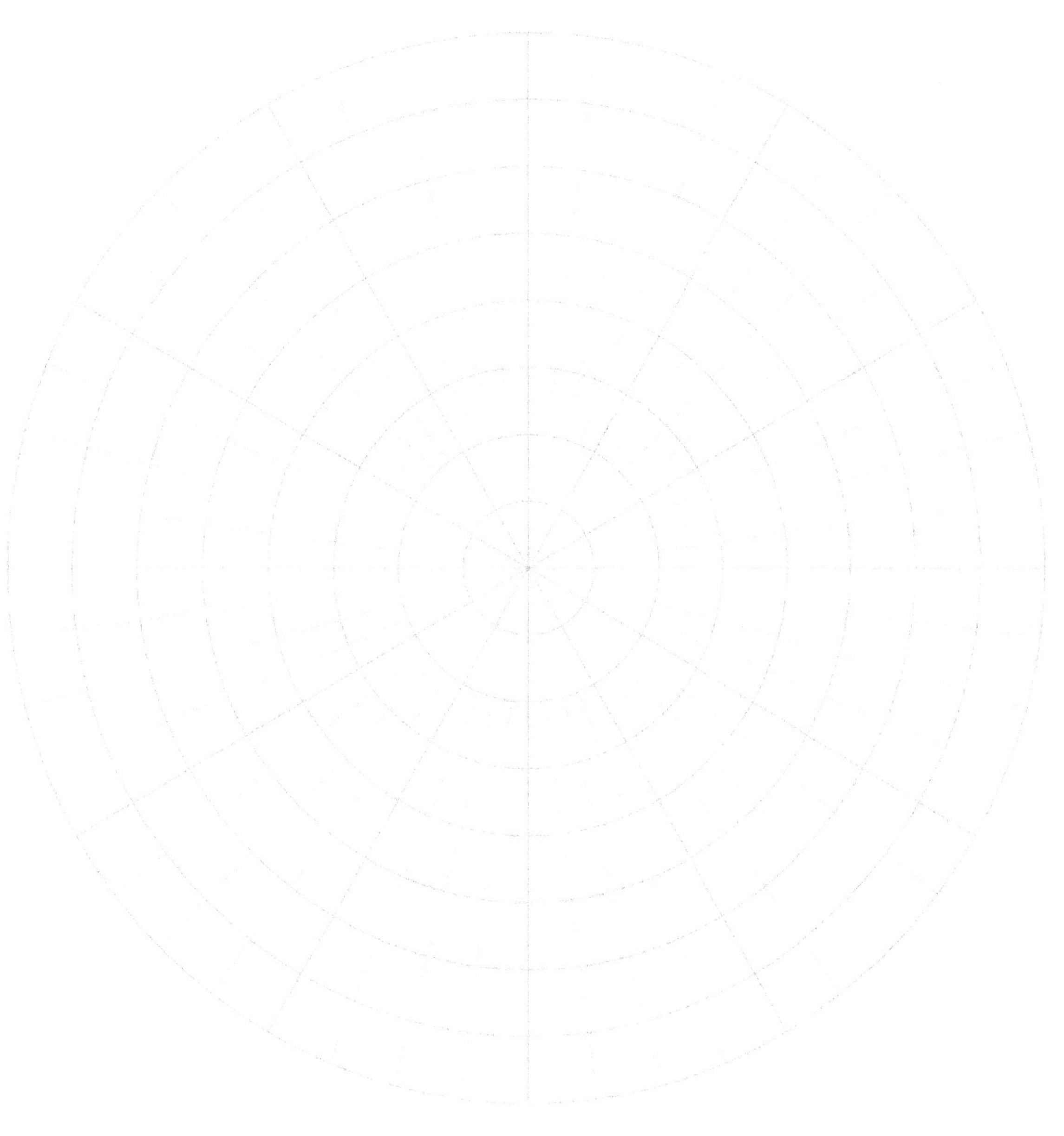

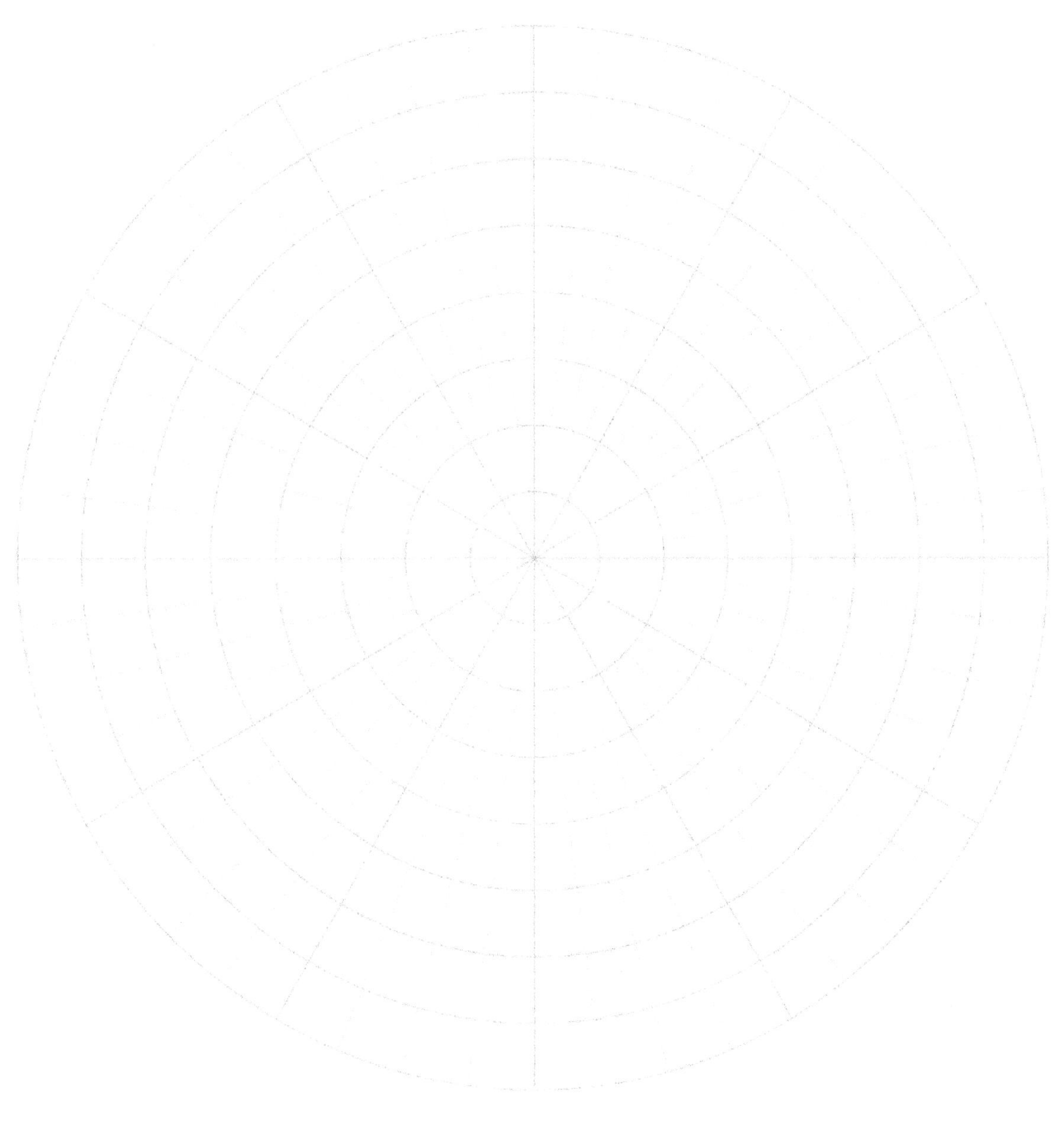

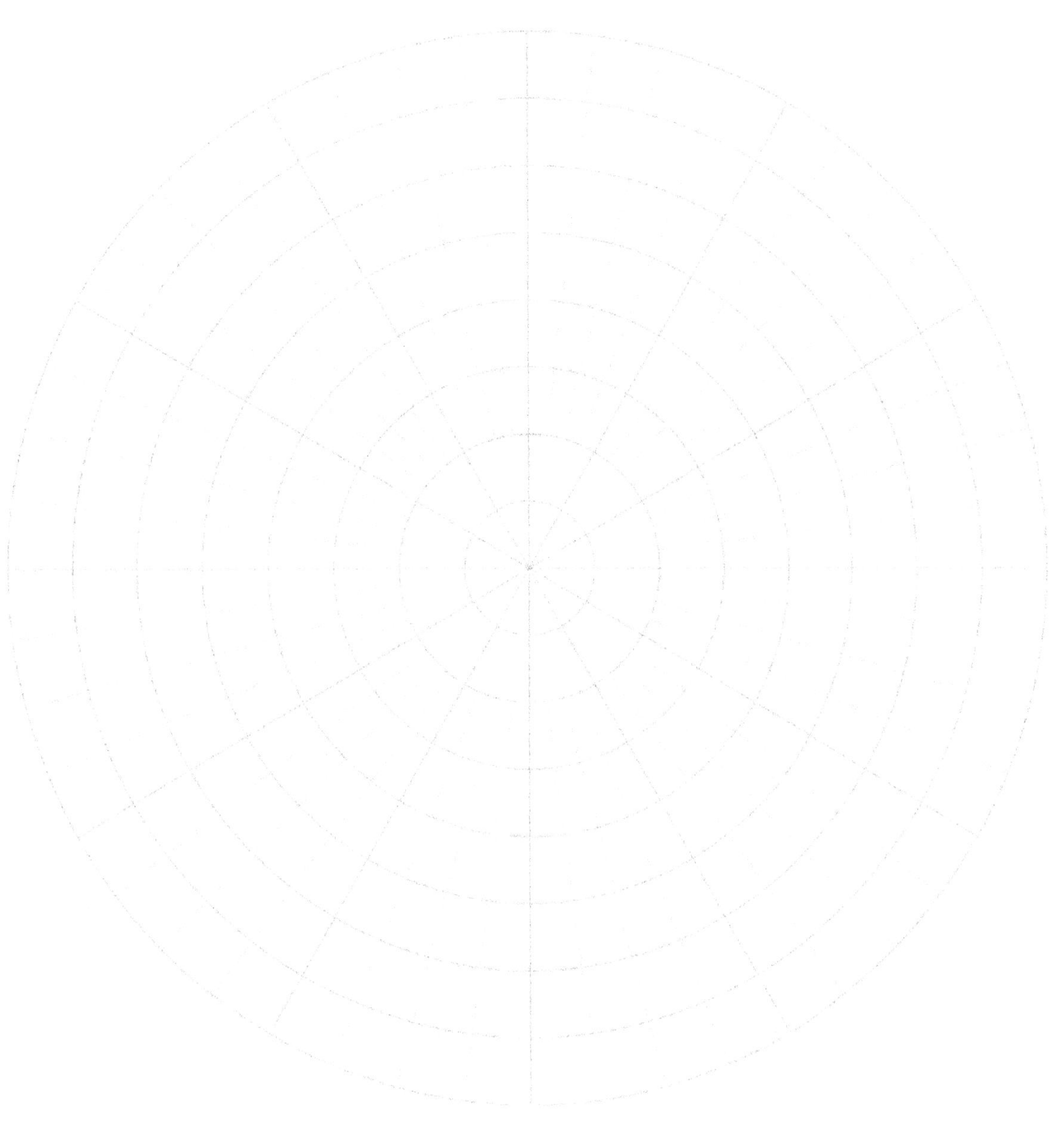

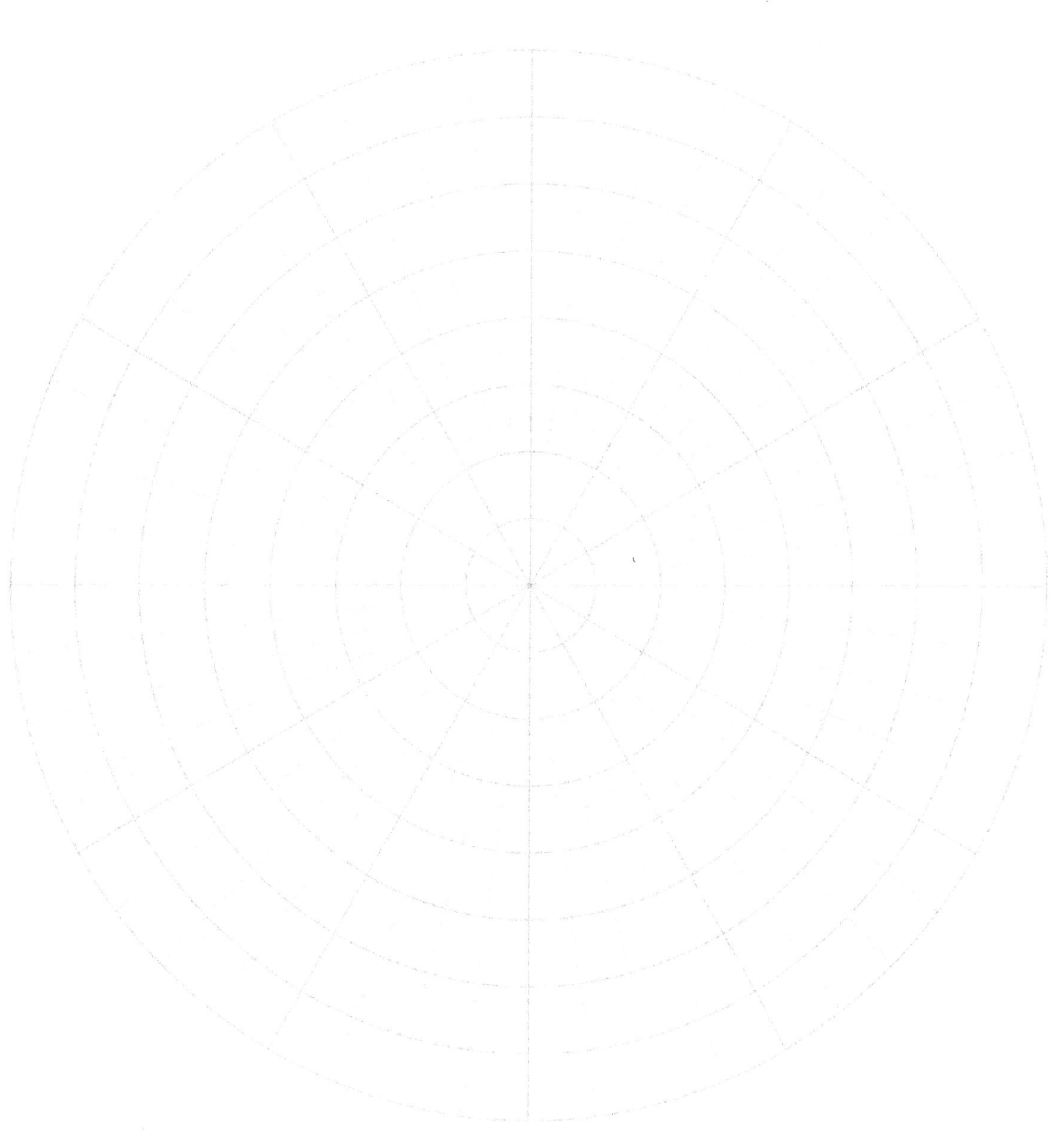

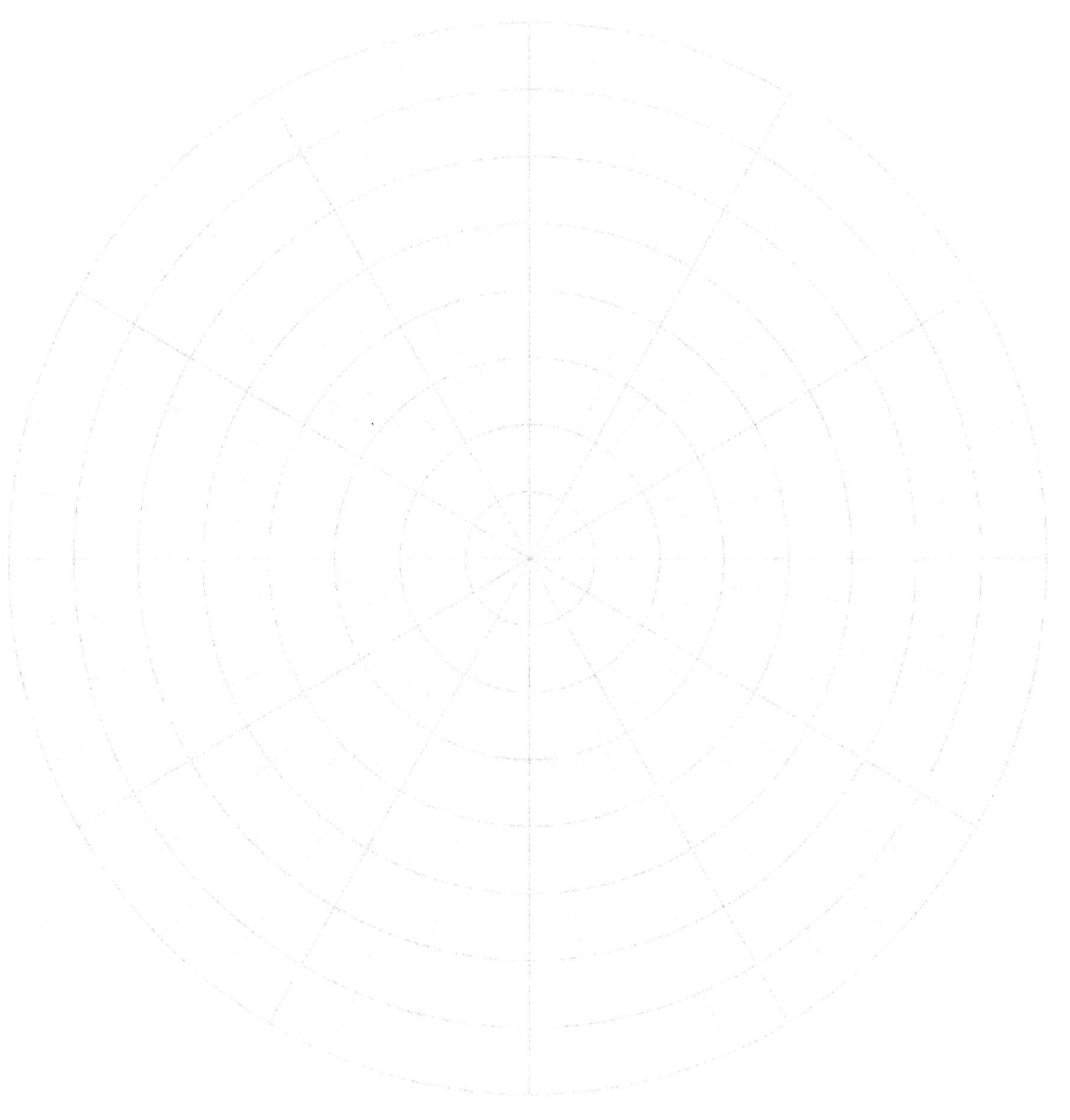

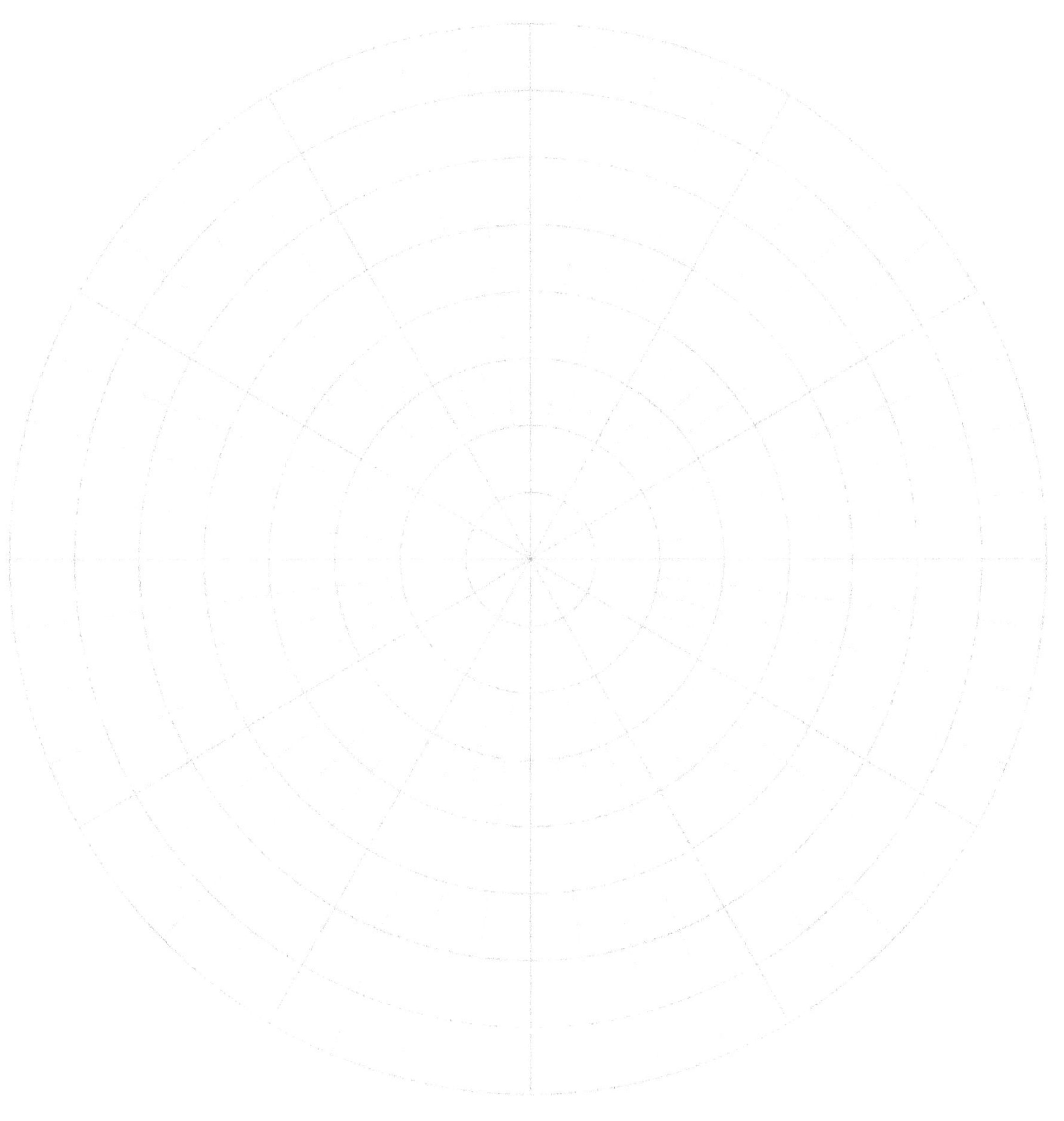

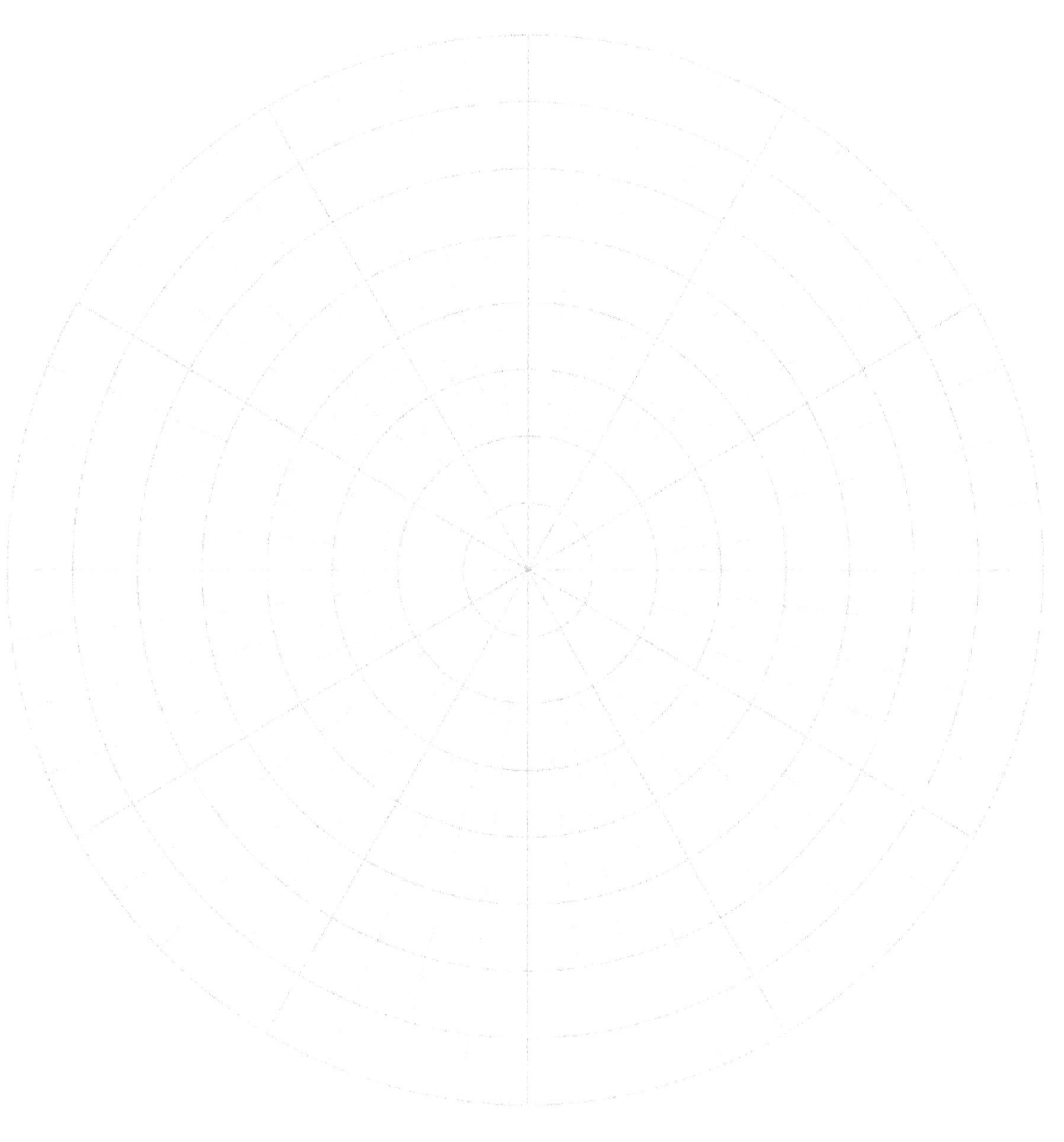

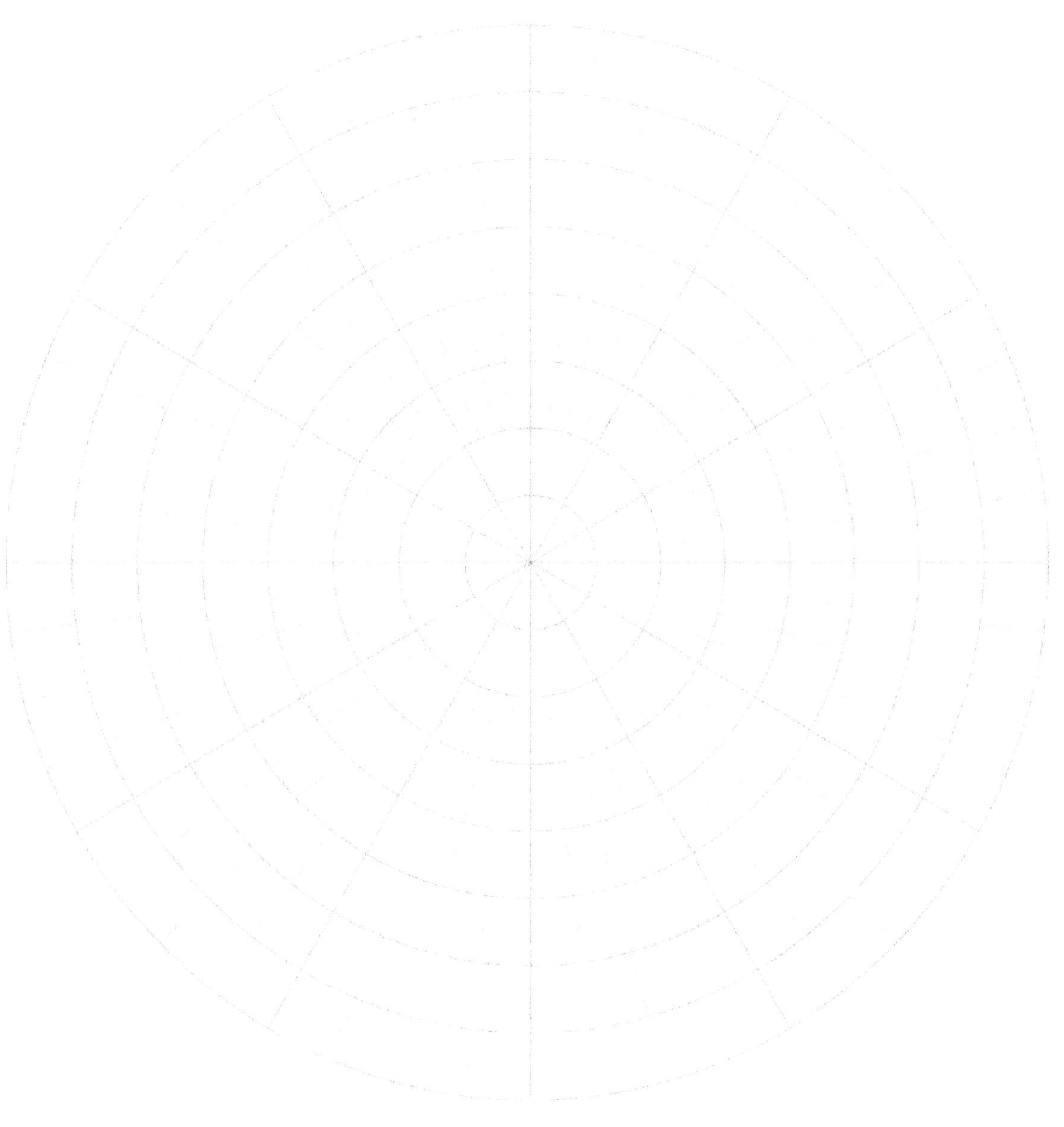

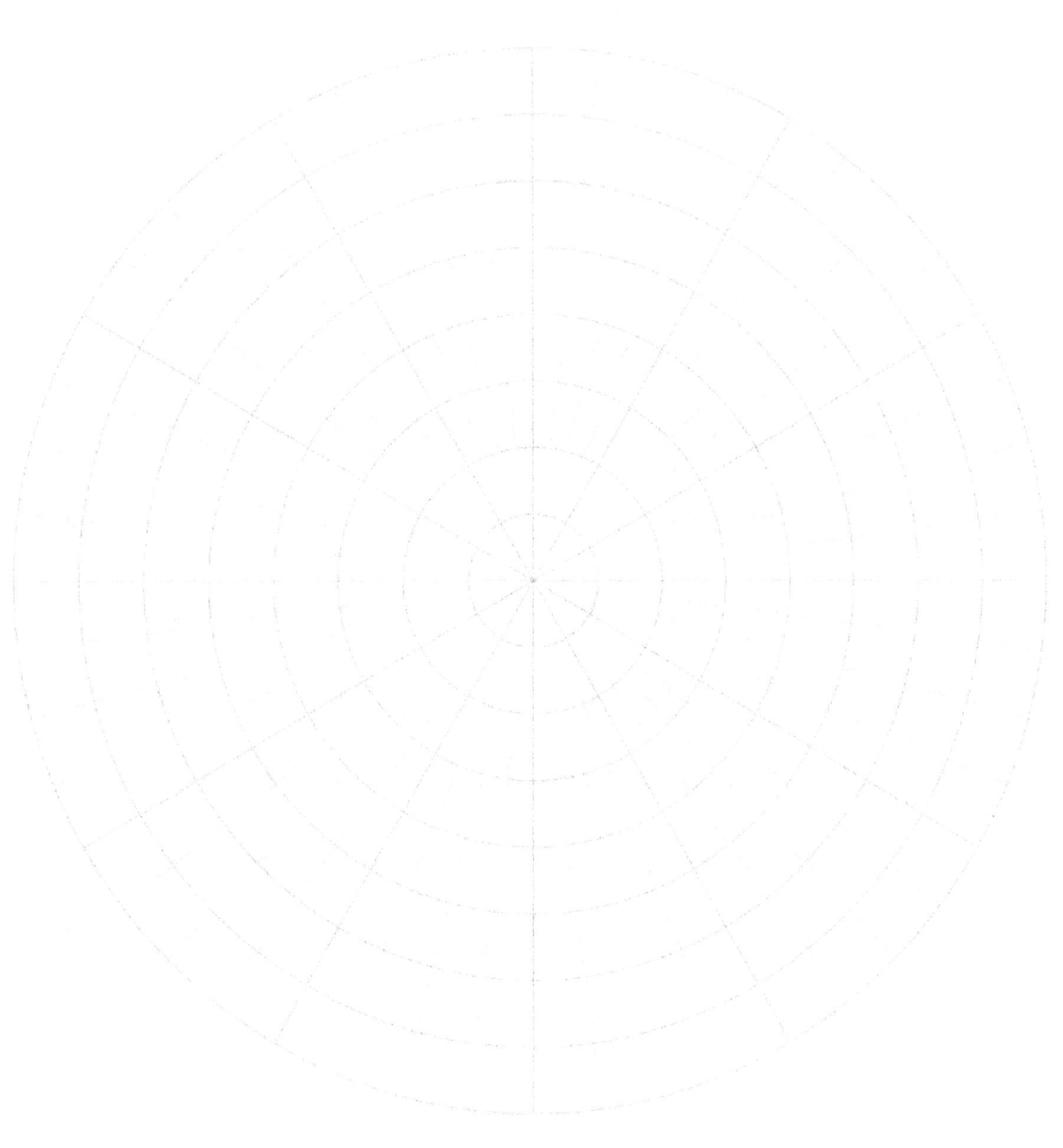

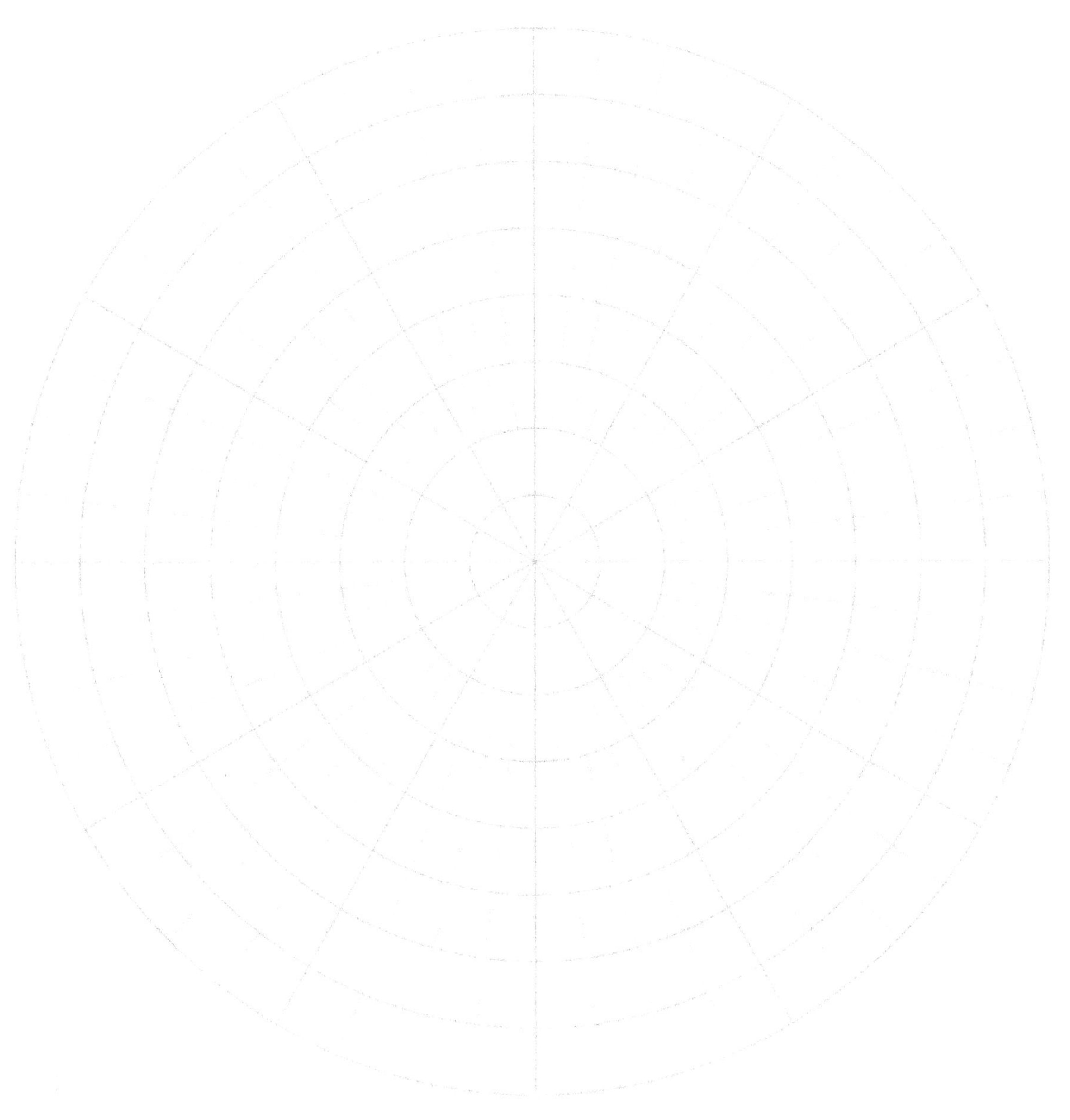

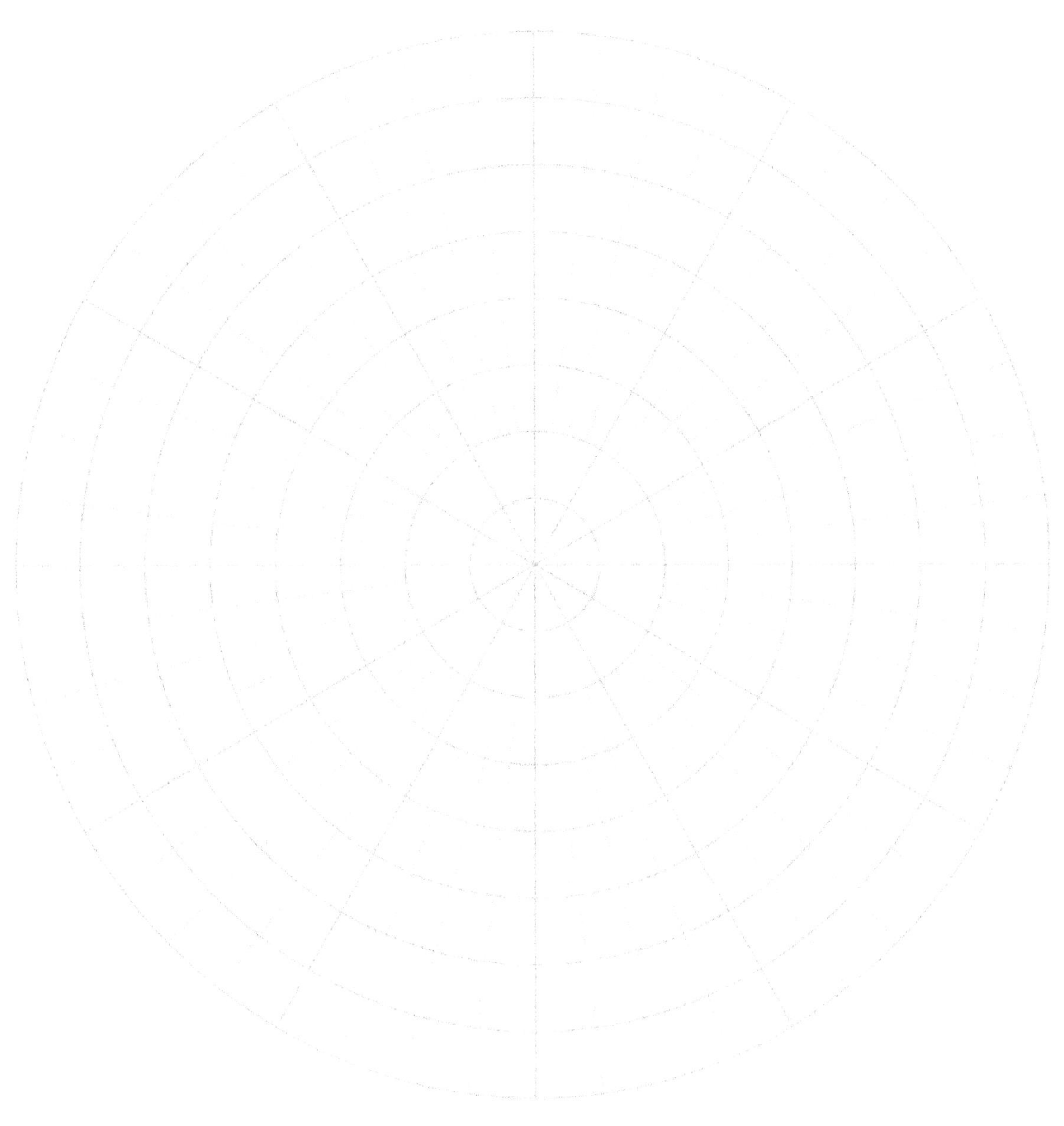

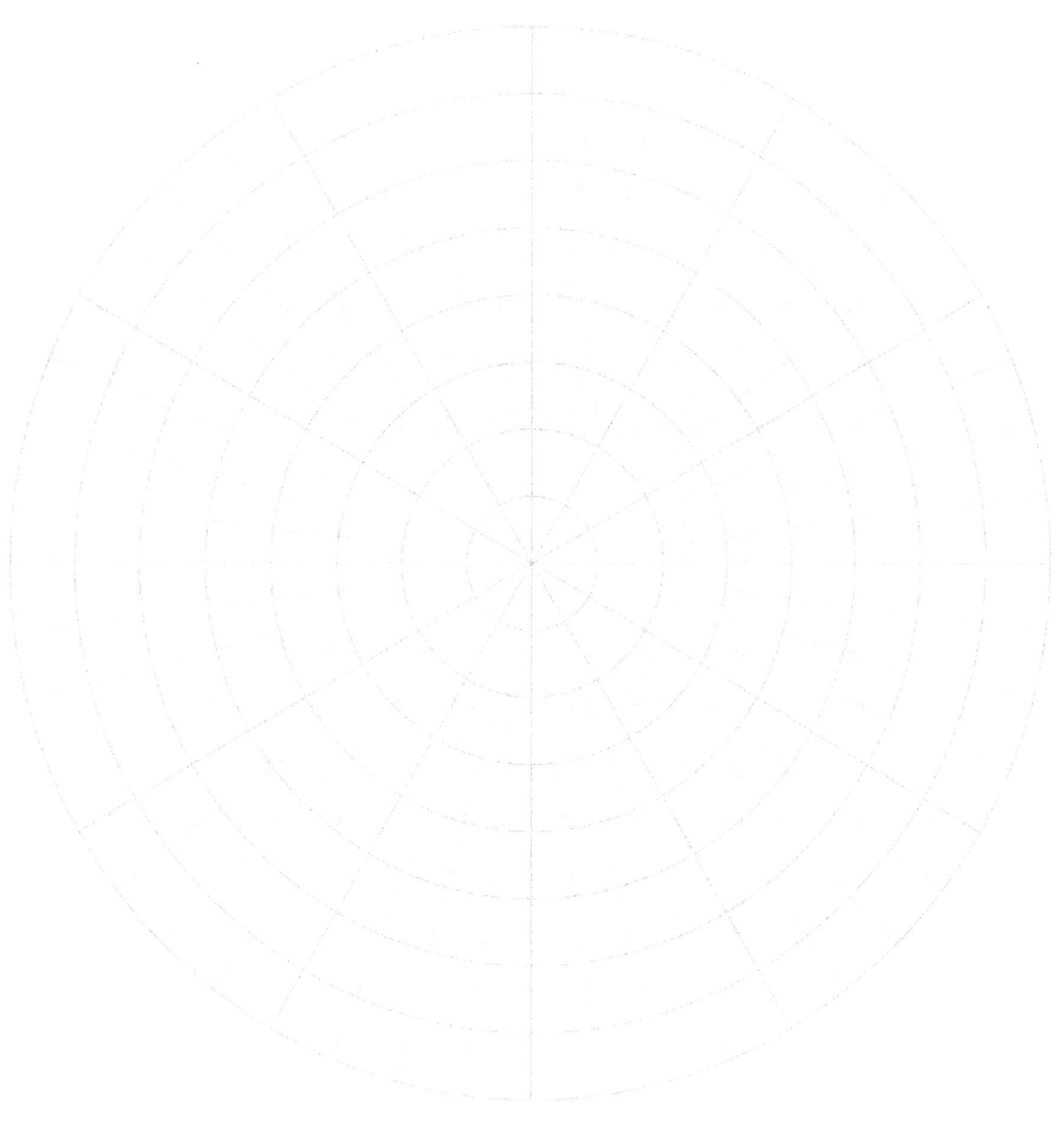

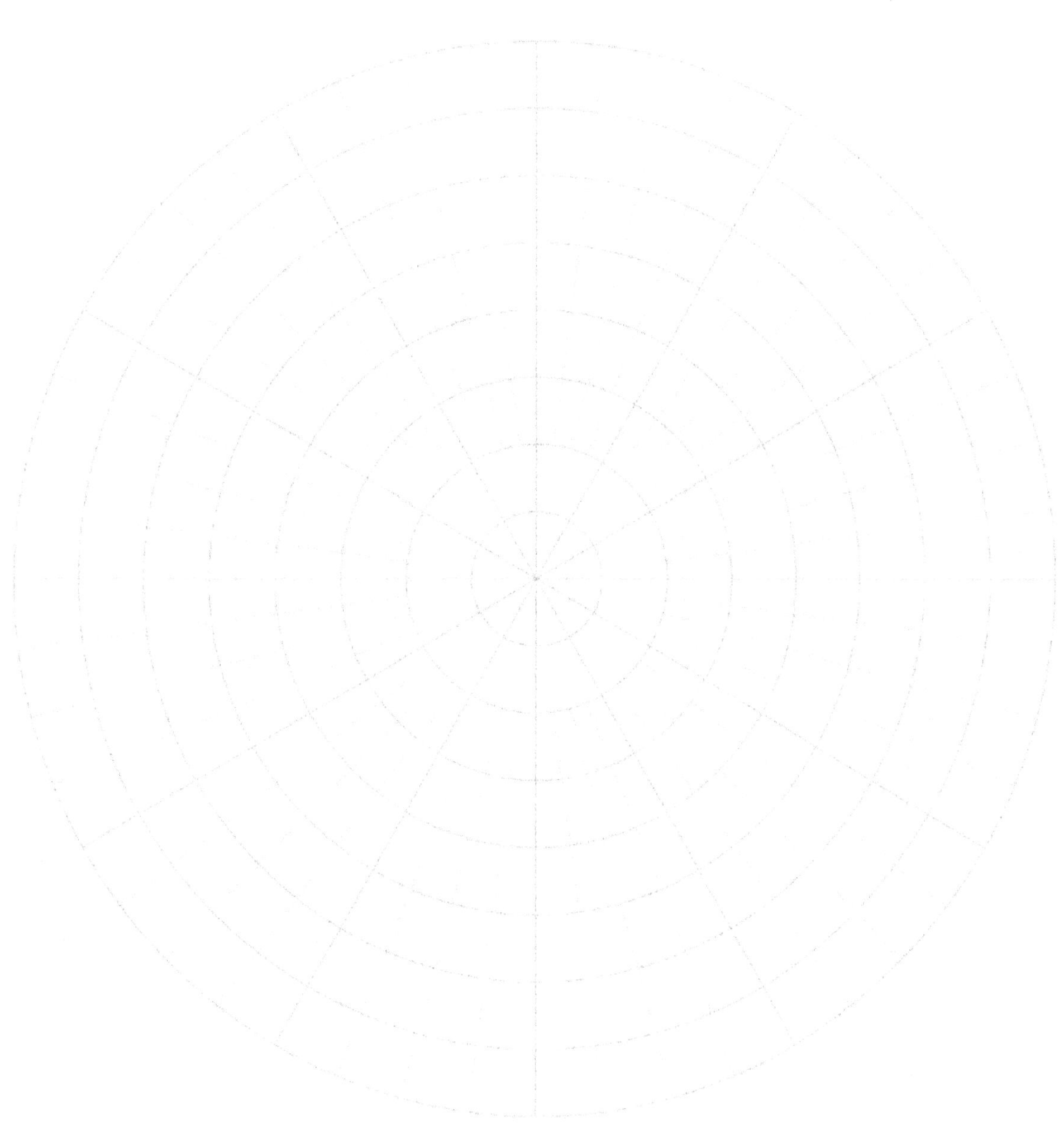

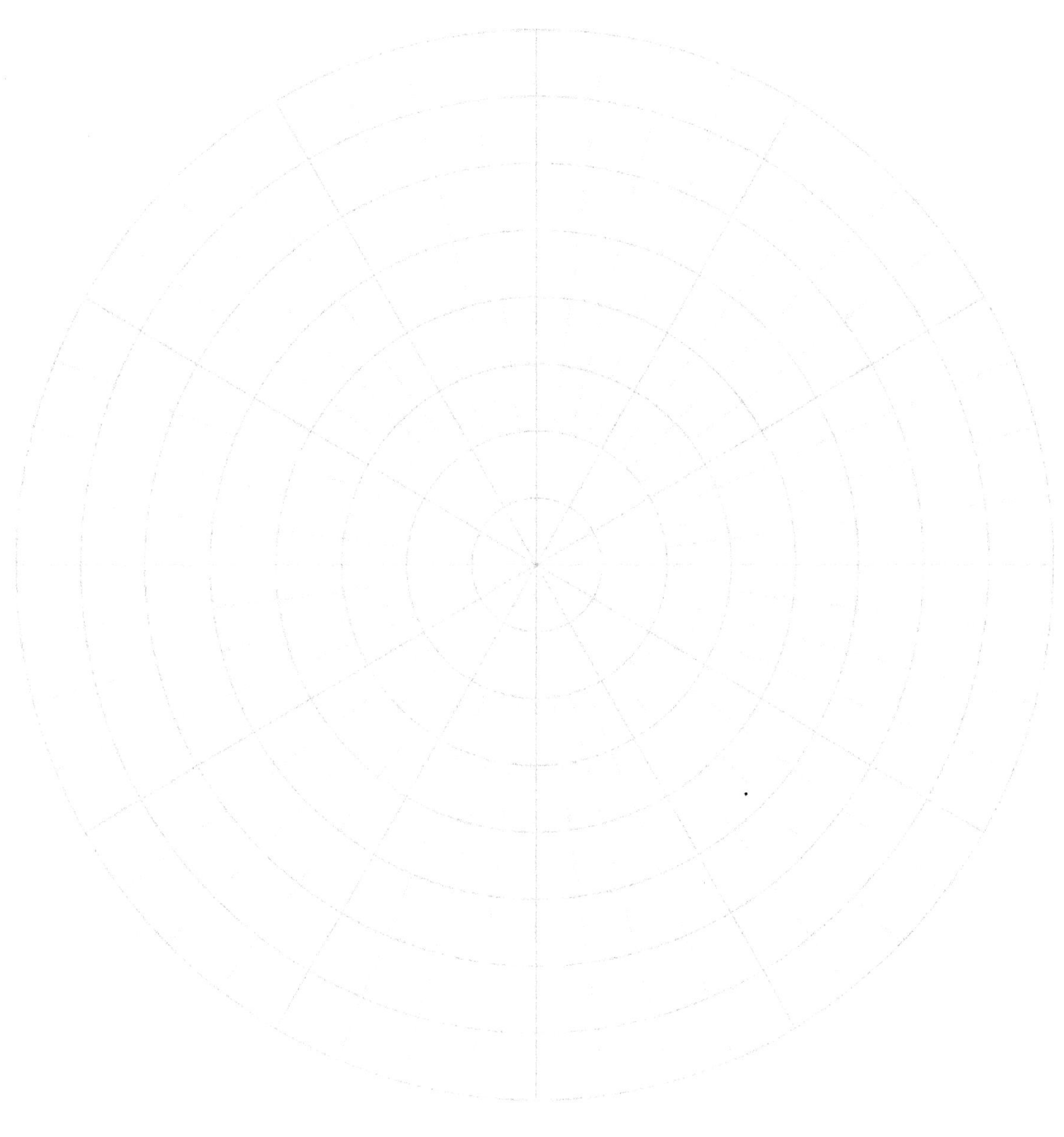

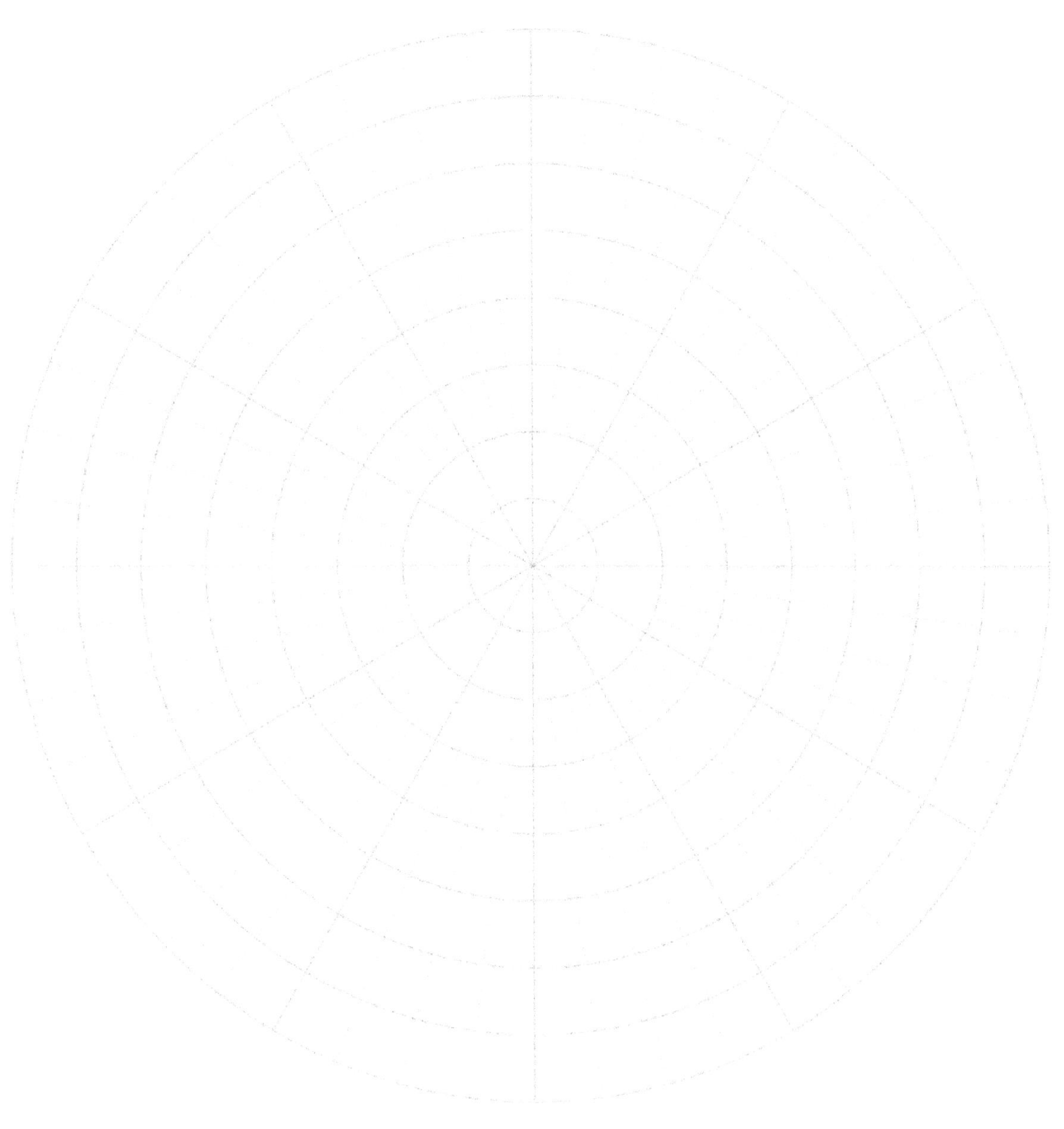

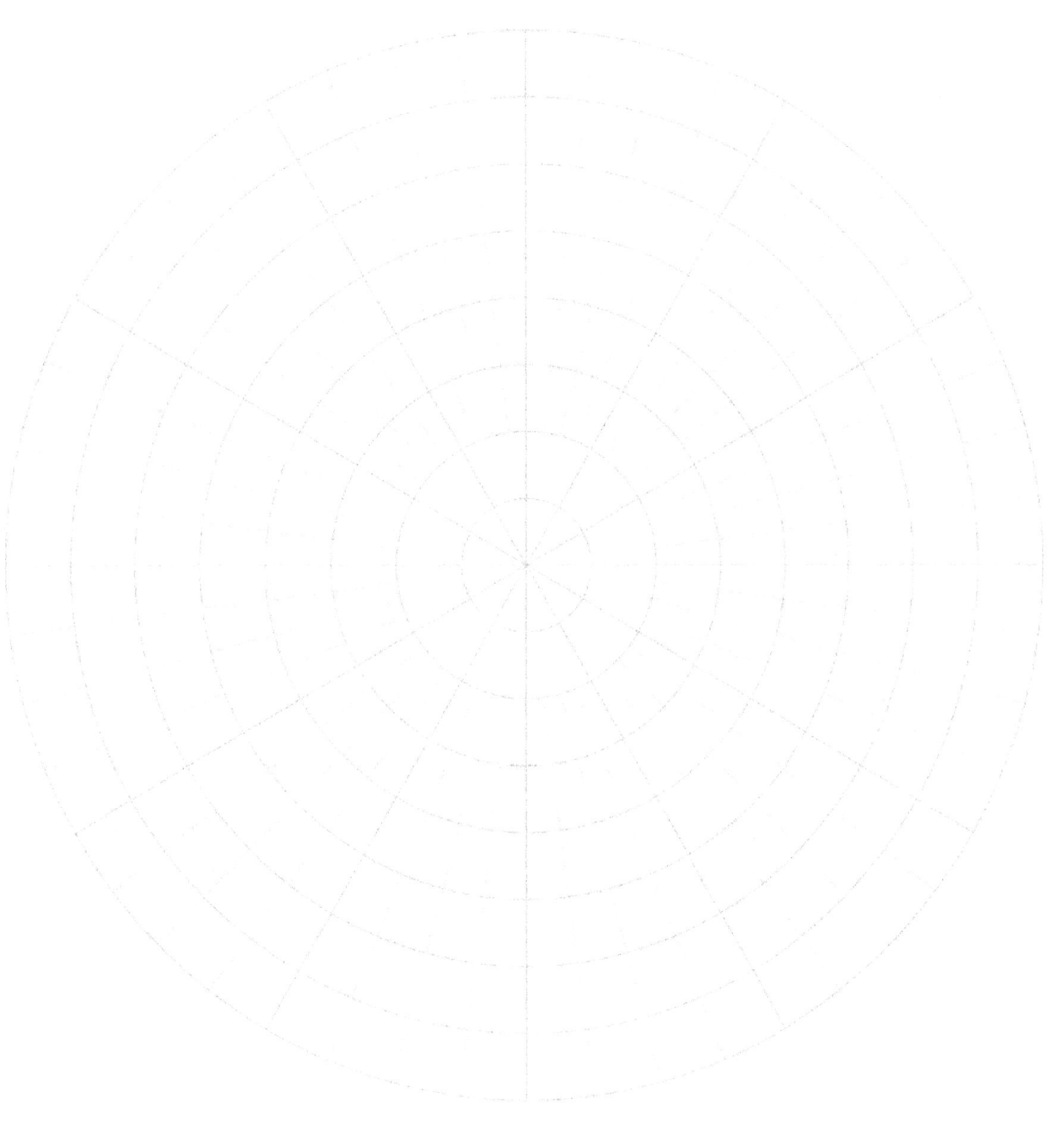

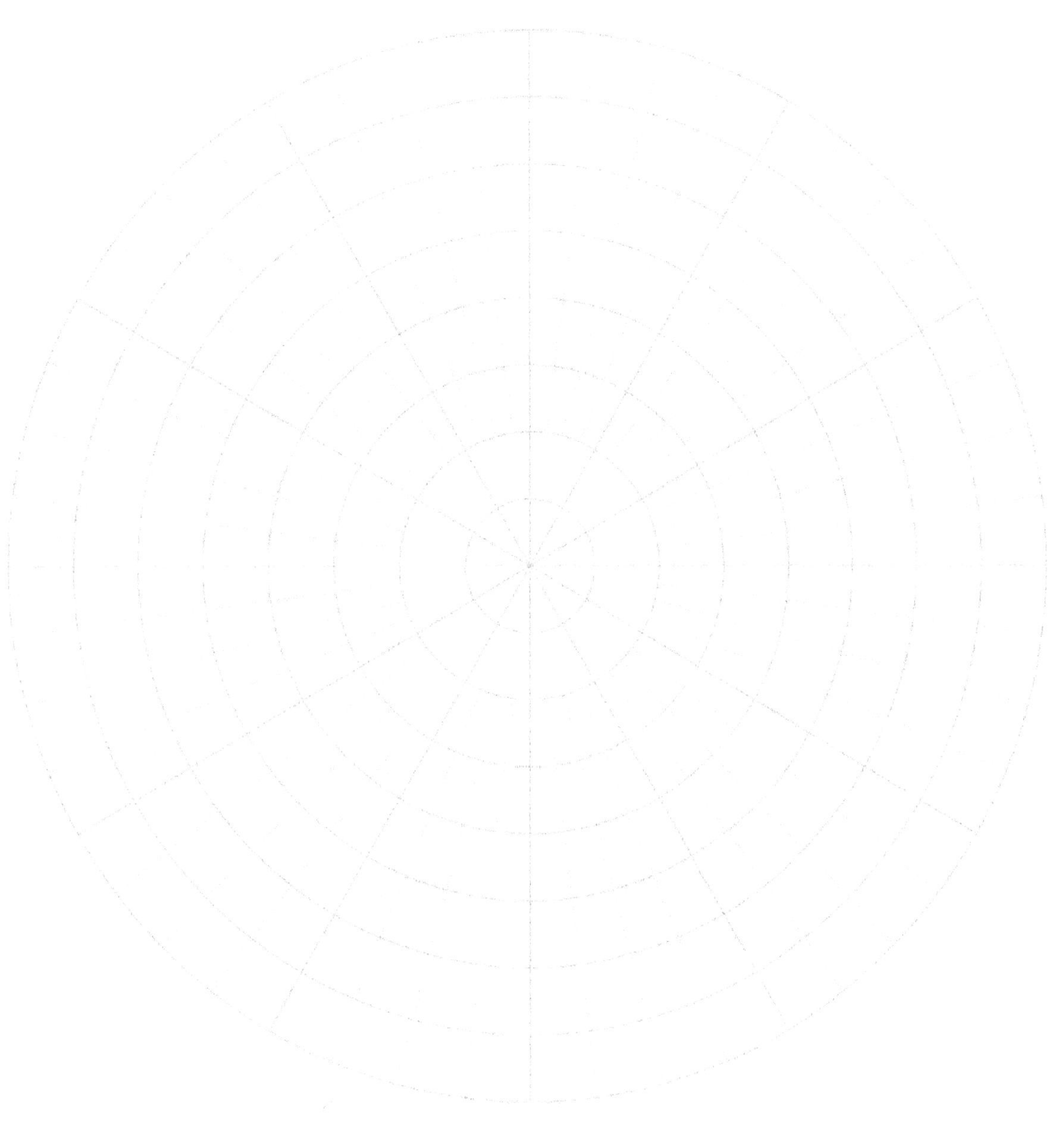

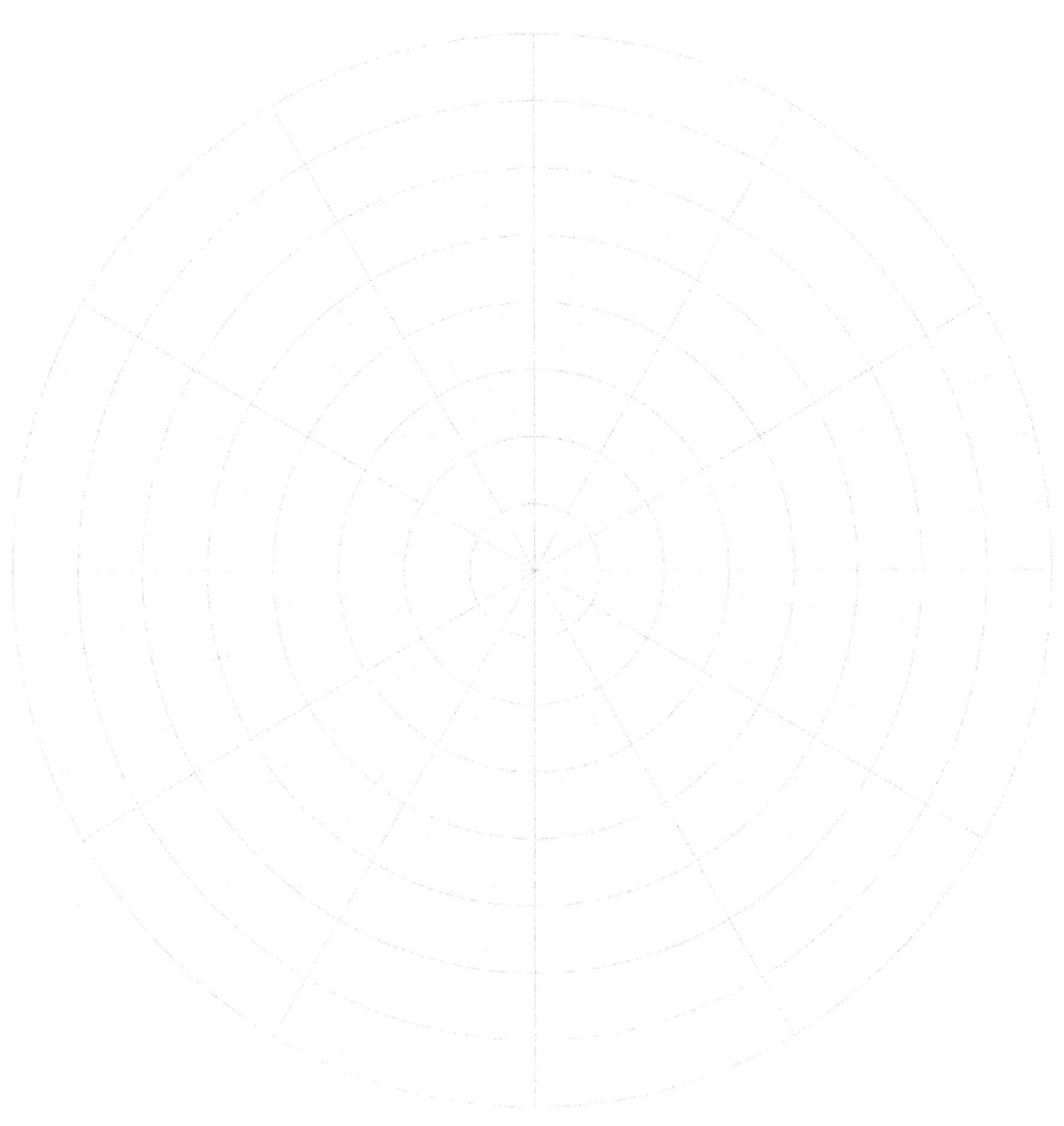

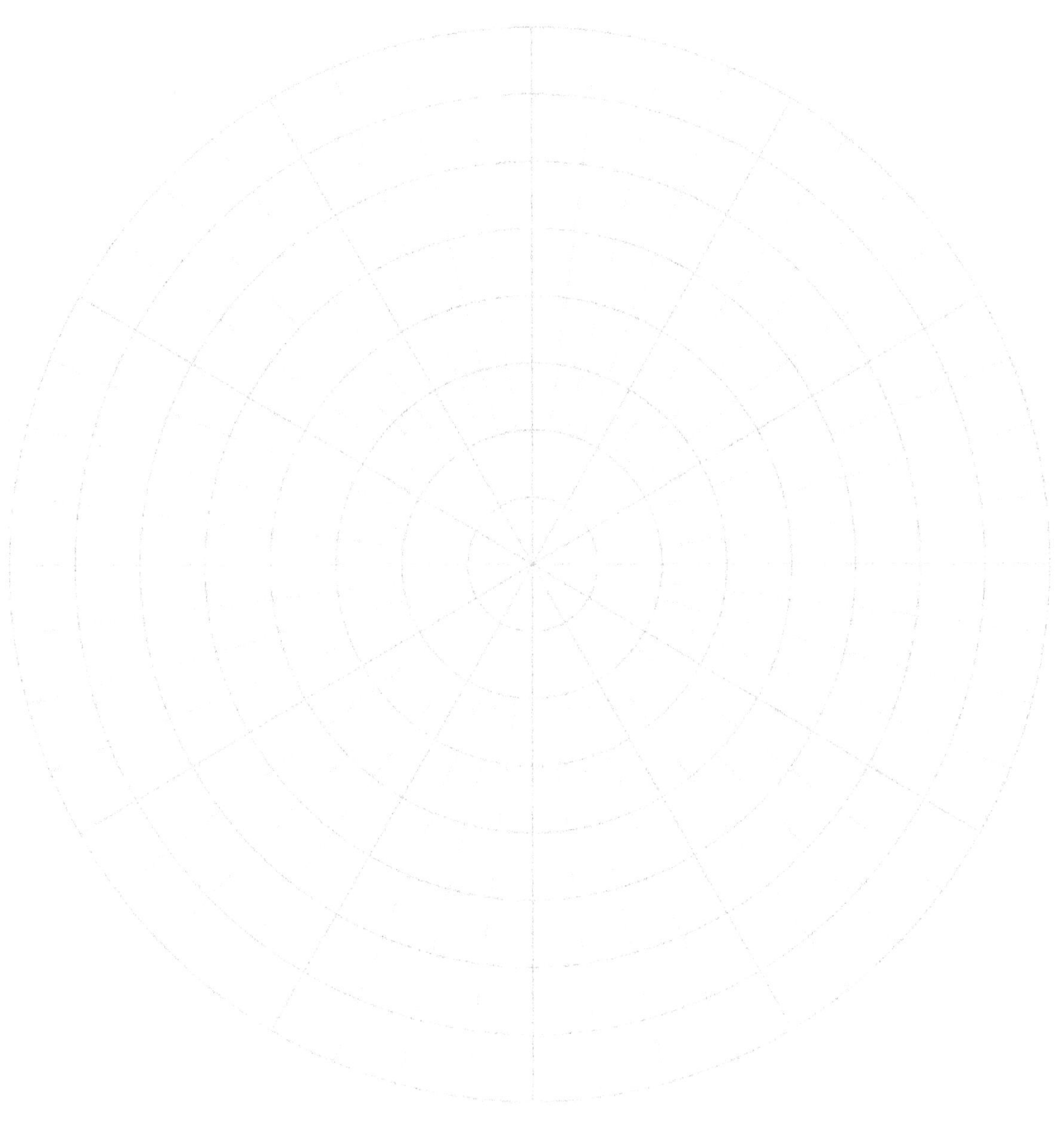

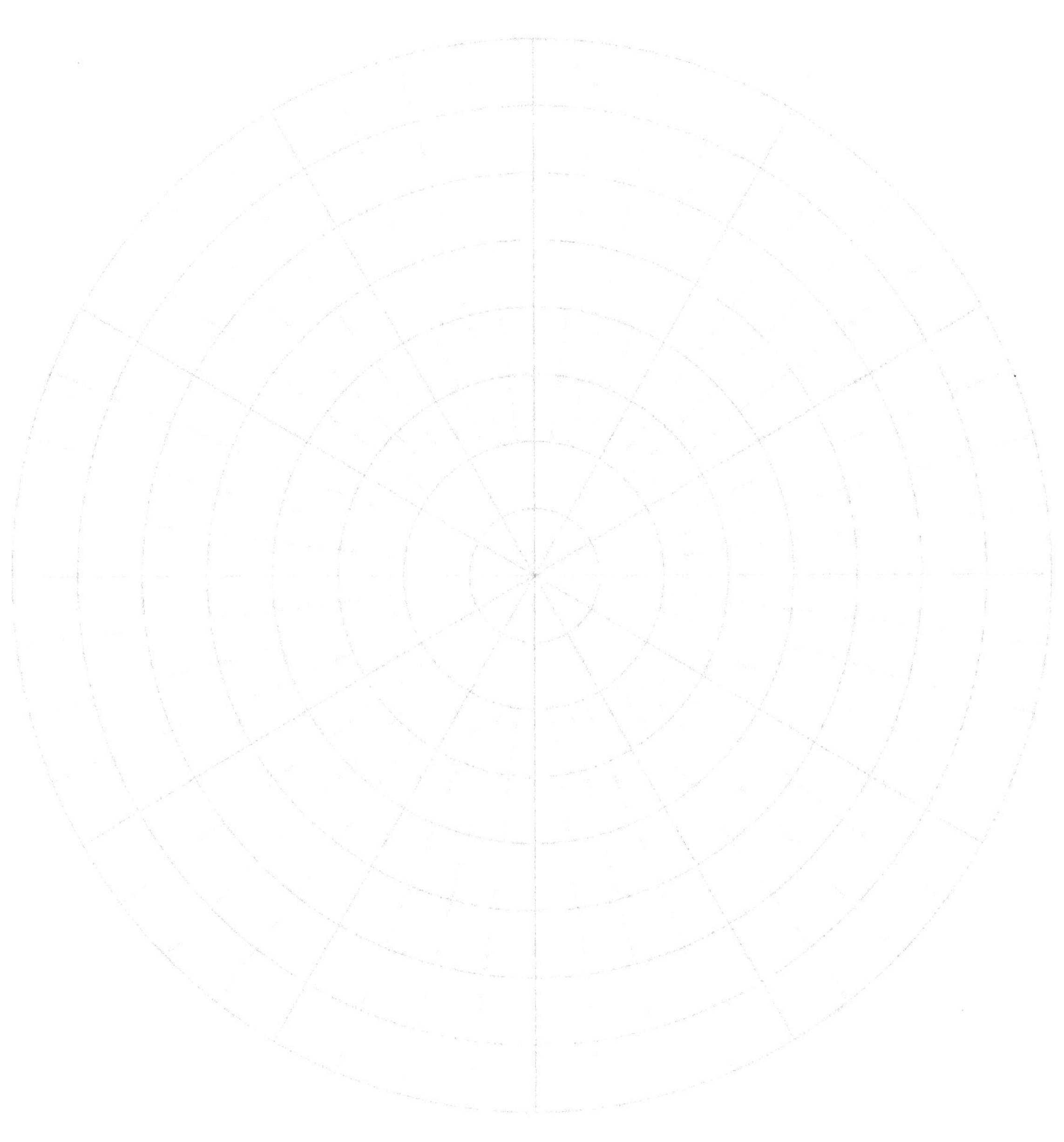

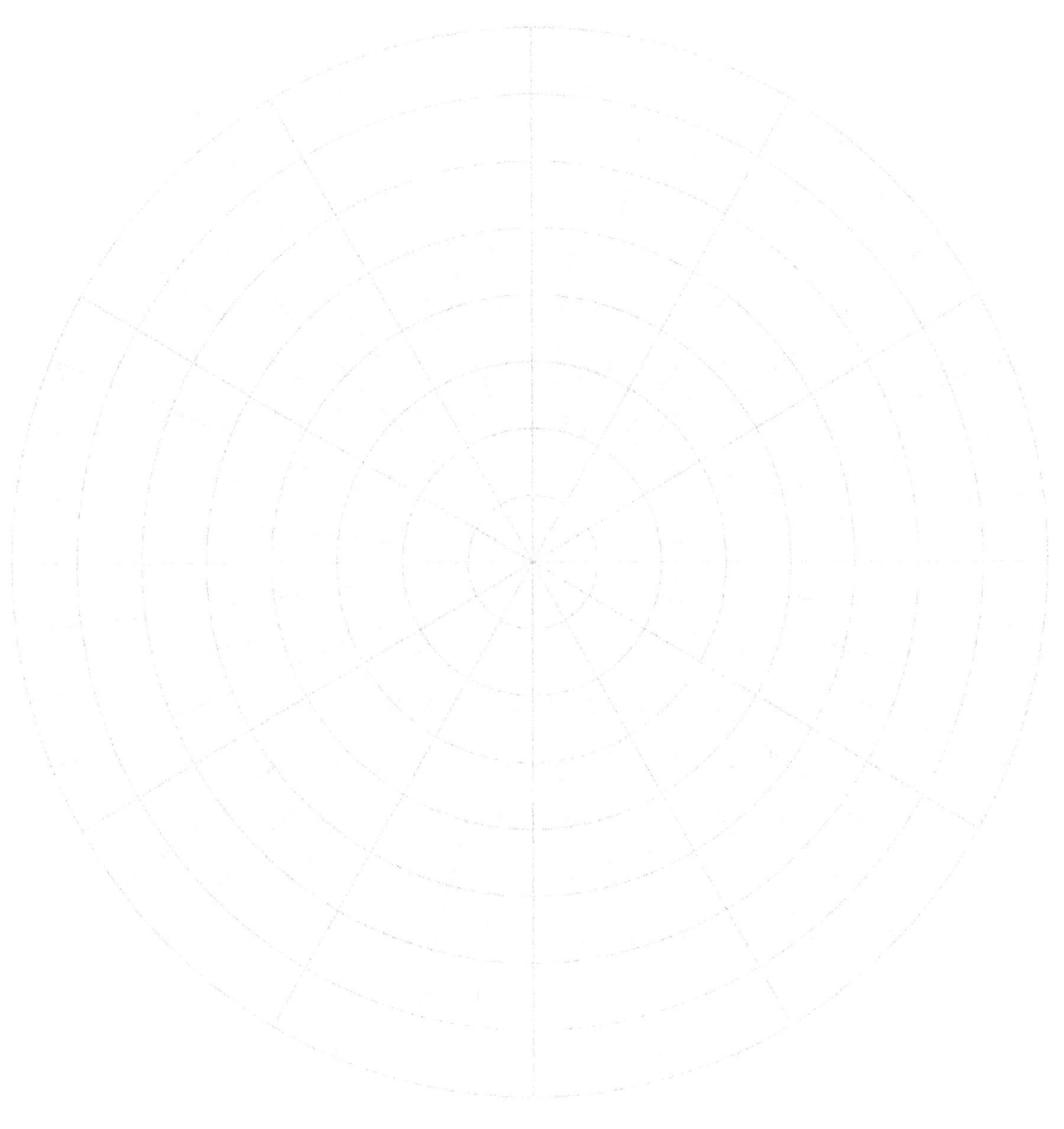

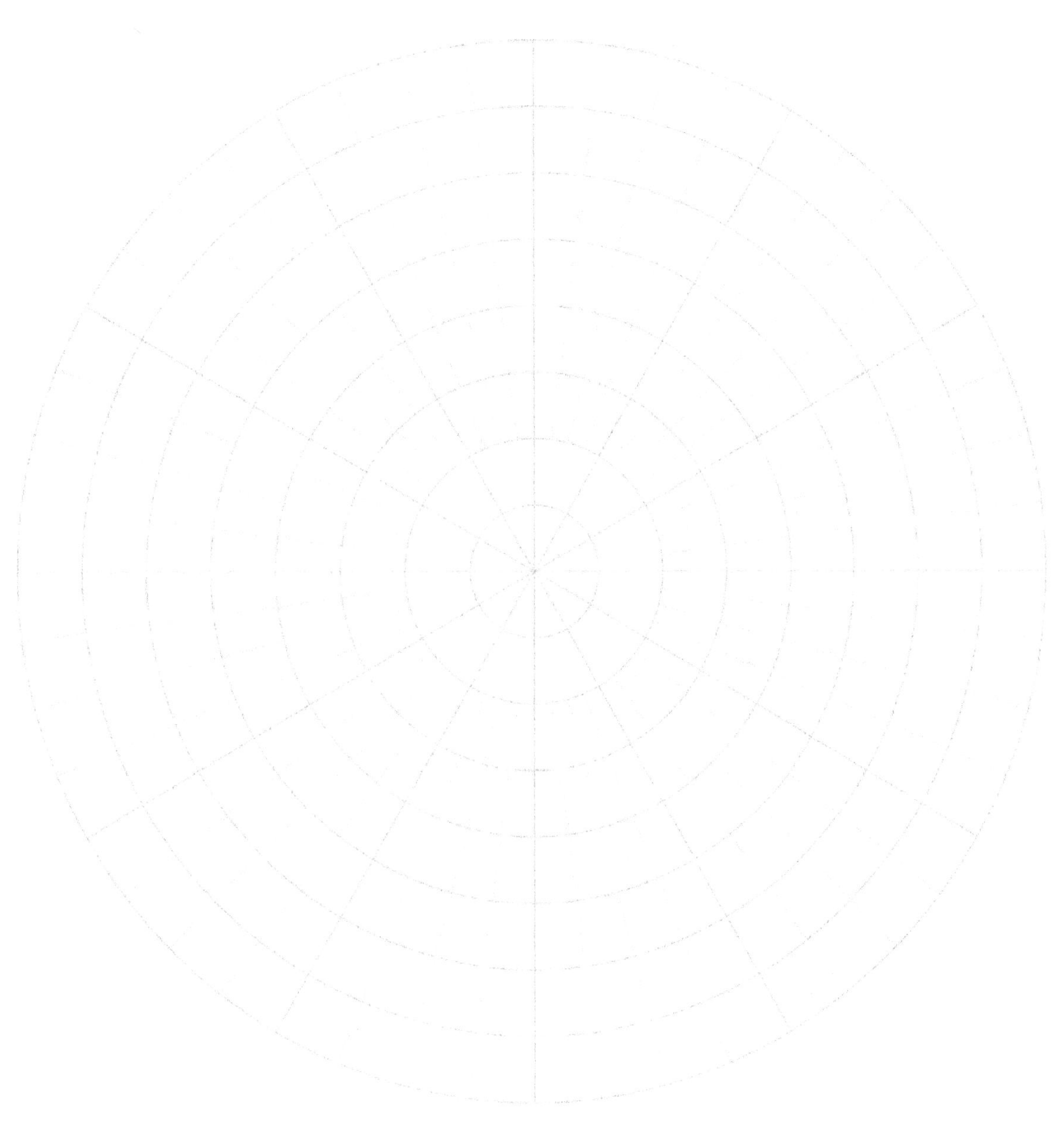

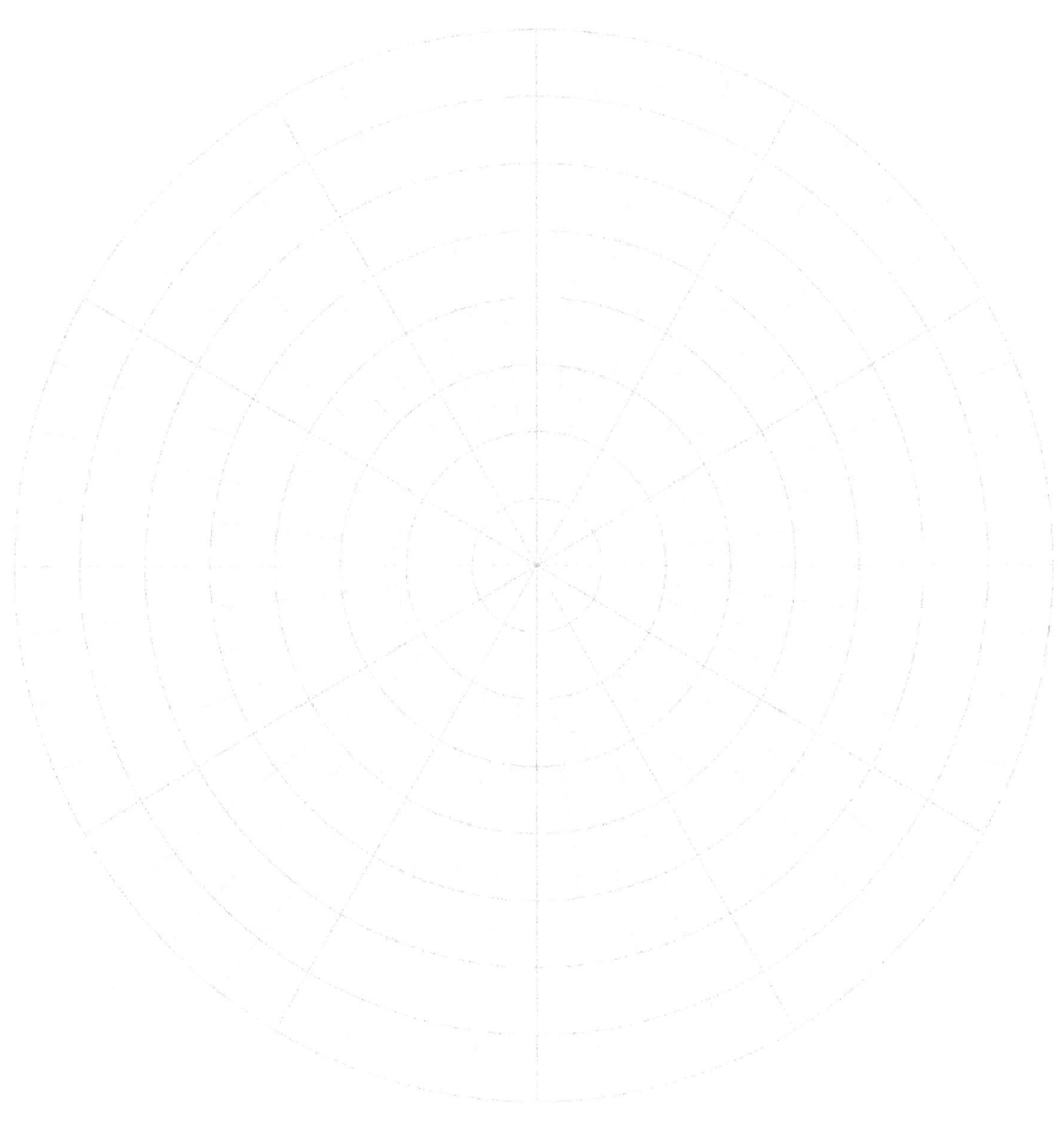

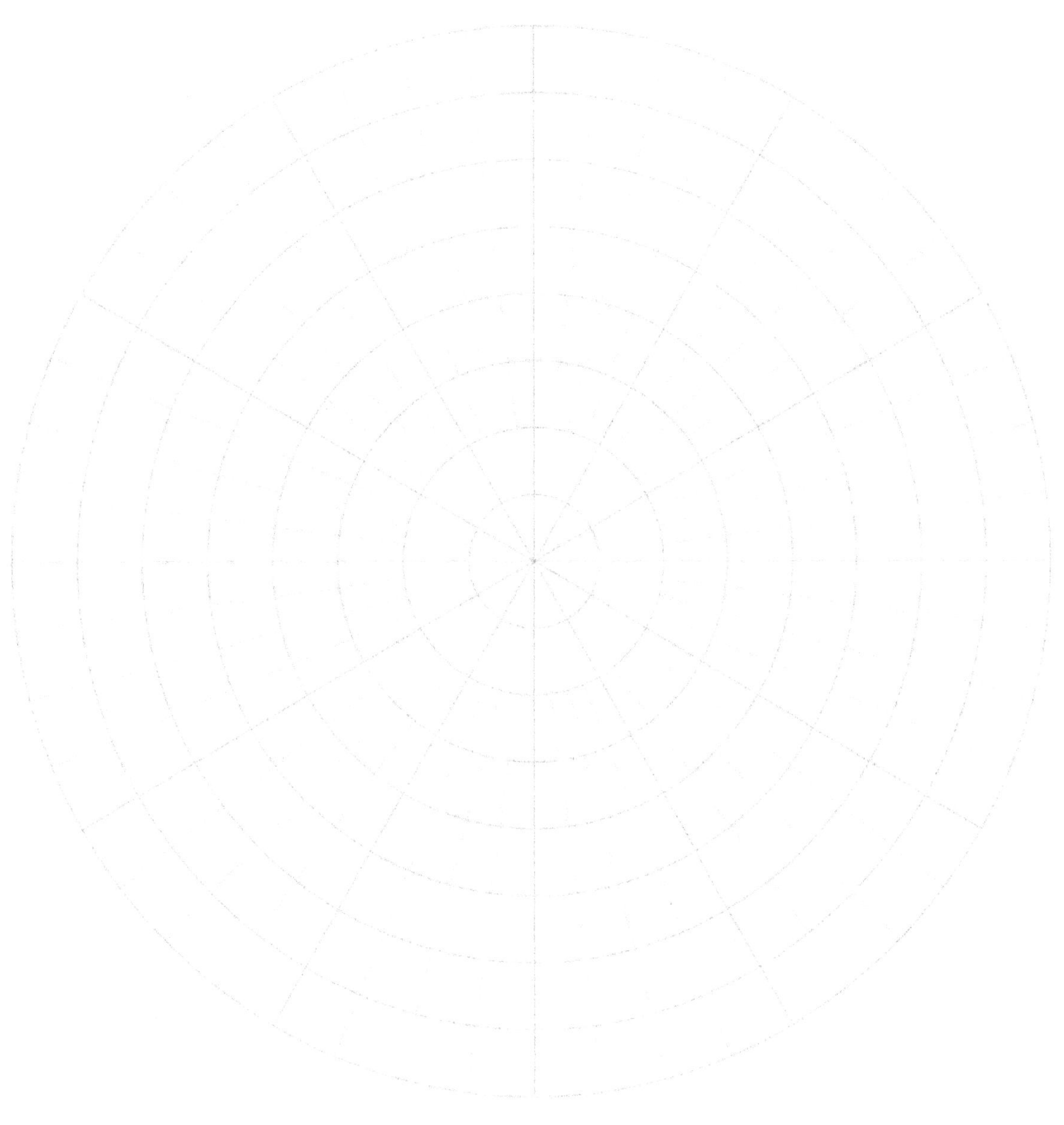

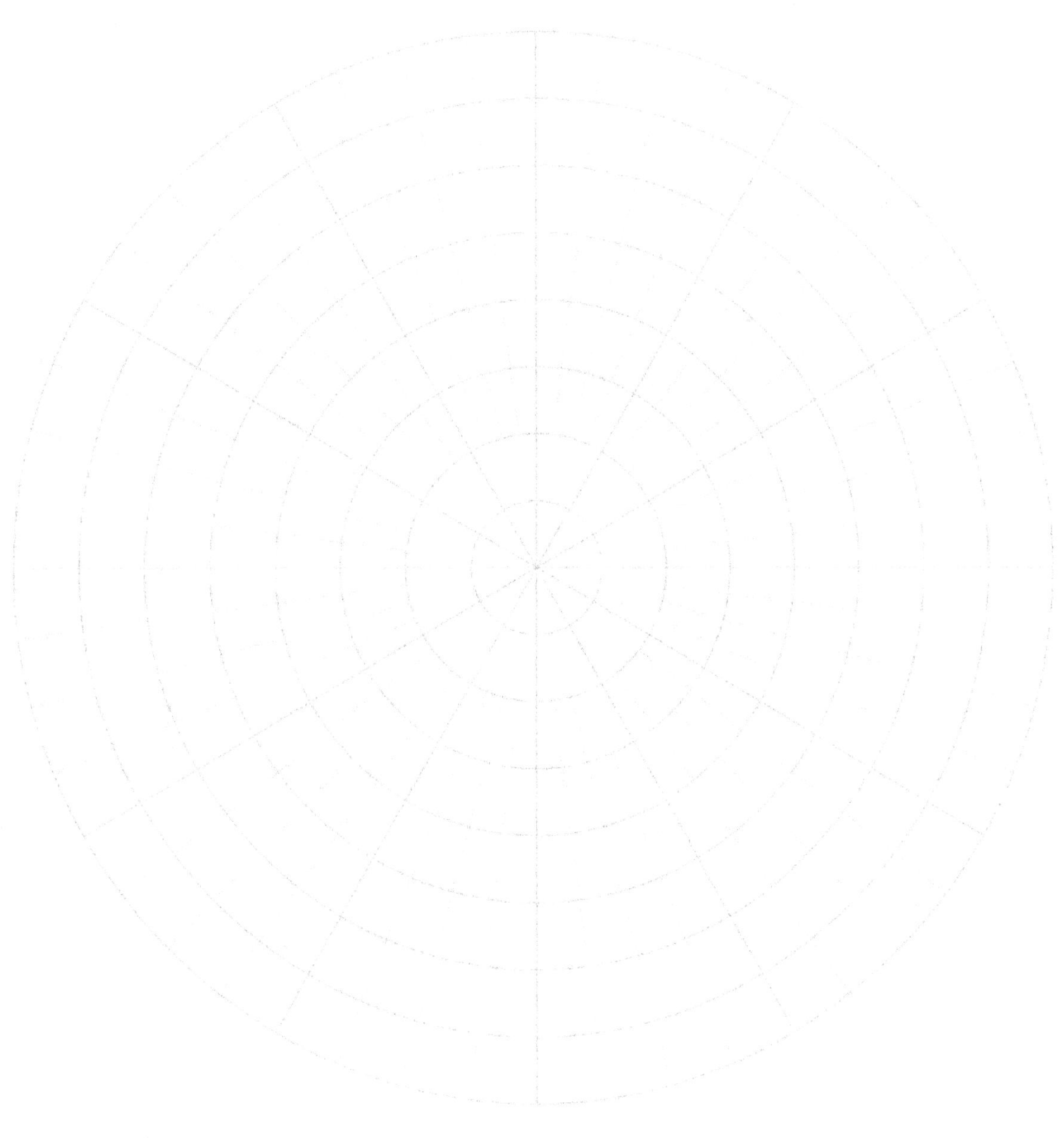

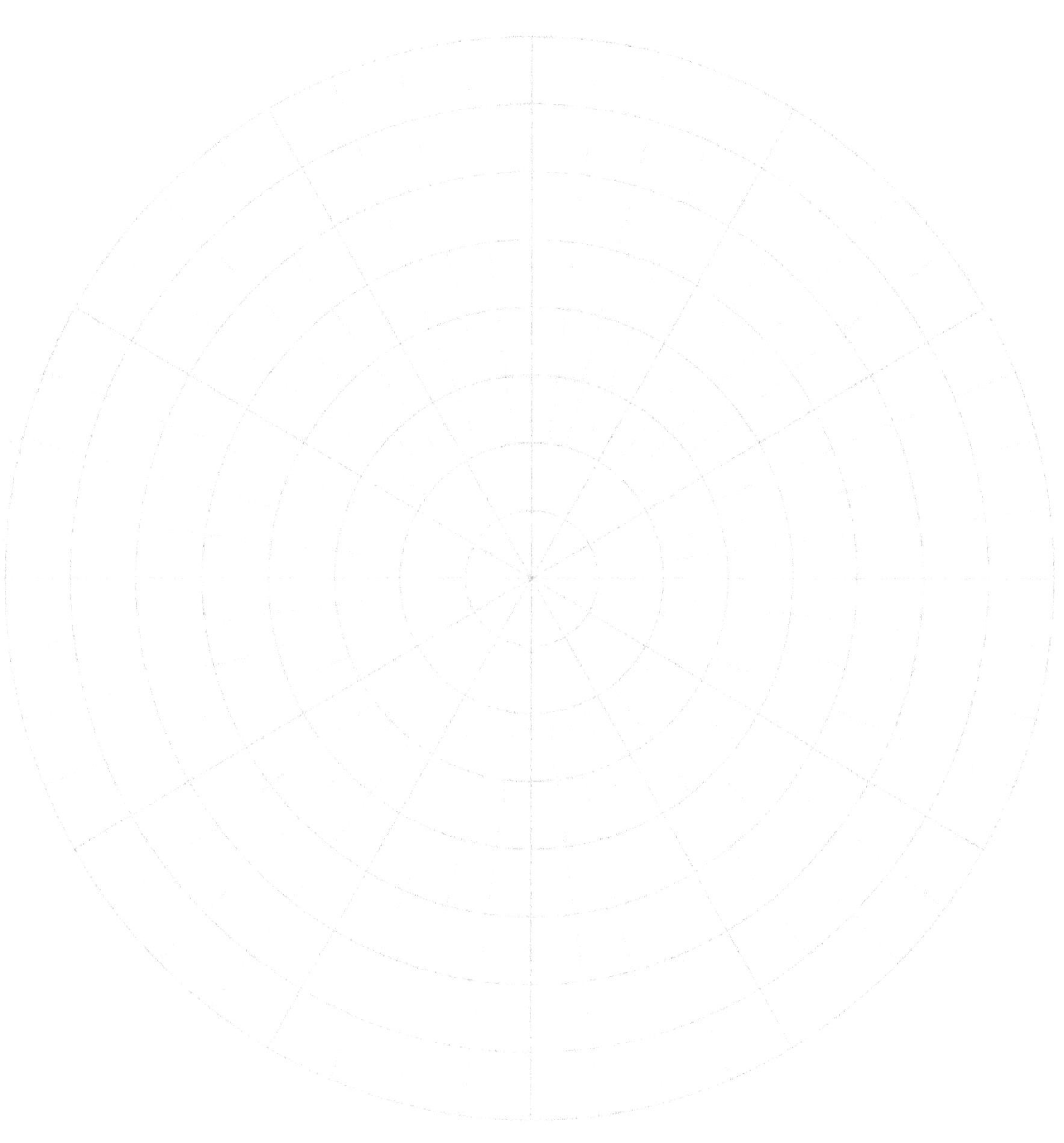

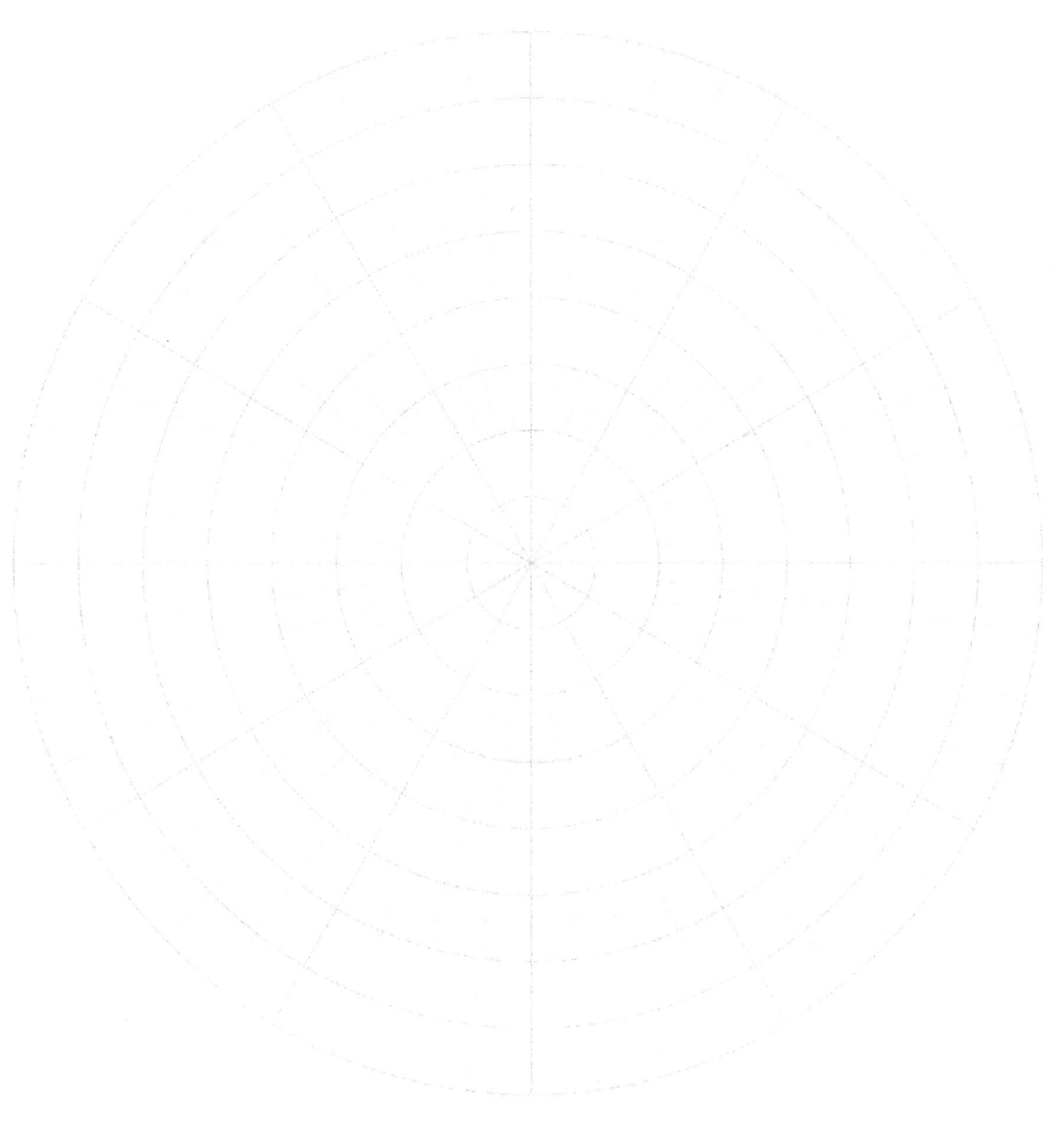

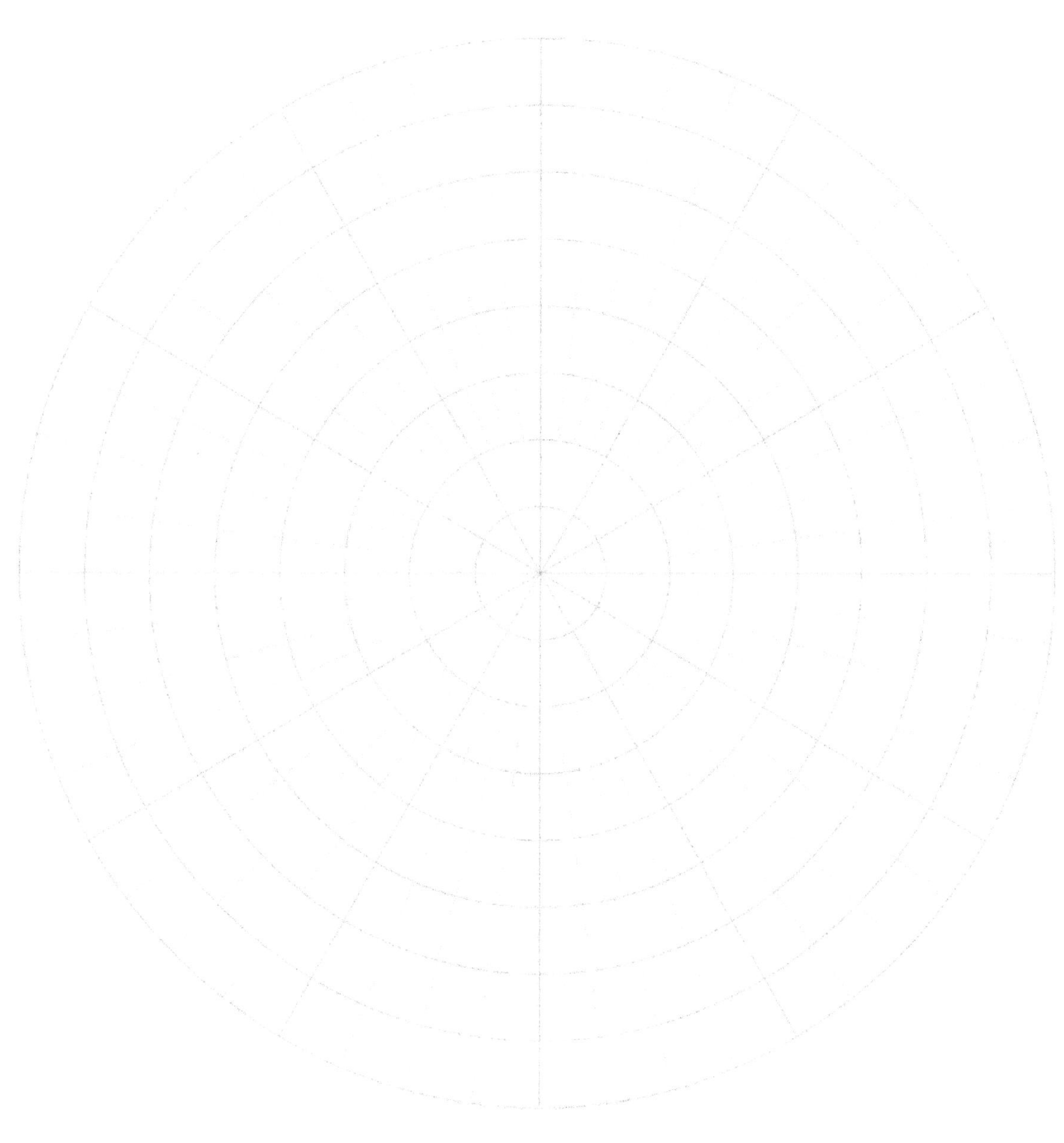

HAVE FUN
AND THANKS